THE VICTORIA HISTORY OF HAMPSHIRE

MAPLEDURWELL

John Hare, Jean Morrin and Stan Waight

VICTORIA
COUNTY
HISTORY

First published 2012

A Victoria County History publication

© The University of London, 2012

All images © Stan Waight and © John Hare except where stated.

ISBN 978 1 905165 89 6

Cover image: *Detail from Langdon's map of Mapledurwell, 1616.*
© Corpus Christi College, Oxford.

Back cover image: *St Mary's church, from the west.*

Typeset in Minion pro by Kerry Whitston

CONTENTS

LIST OF ILLUSTRATIONS

LIST OF MAPS AND PLANS

Map

FOREWORD

THE IDEA OF a national series of town and parish histories for every county in England was first mooted at Queen Victoria's Diamond Jubilee in 1897 and was dedicated to her. In 2012, Her Majesty the Queen graciously agreed to the rededication of the project to mark her own Diamond Jubilee.

The Victoria County History is the greatest publishing project in English local history. Hampshire was the first county to be completed in 1912 but its parish histories concentrated on leading families, the Church of England and local charities. I am delighted and proud that Hampshire is now also the first county to undertake a complete revision in the modern VCH style which includes the social, economic and religious history of the ordinary people of the parish. This very readable, fascinating and well illustrated history of Mapledurwell is the first fruit of this ambition to be published in printed form. Mapledurwell is a picturesque rural village with attractive timber-framed cottages, the oldest of which dates back to the 15th century. The parish itself has been transformed since the publication of the original VCH from an agricultural community to a commuter village with only one working farm.

This history has been researched and written by local volunteers, especially Stan Waight, led by Jean Morrin of the University of Winchester, with help from professional historians including John Hare and Michael Hicks. The manor of Mapledurwell has been owned by Corpus Christi College, Oxford for nearly 500 years and this history has been greatly enhanced by study of records in the College's extensive archive. The Hampshire volunteers continue to research eleven other parishes in the Basingstoke area, including the town itself.

Financial help has come from the Marc Fitch Fund, the Charlotte Bonham-Carter Charitable Fund, The Bulldog Trust, the University of Winchester and individuals. Particularly welcome have been the donations from Mapledurwell Parish Council and several villagers.

I commend this scholarly parish history to you and hope, with more help and support, it will be followed by many more, until the detailed history of the whole of the historic county of Hampshire is brought fully up to date.

Mary Fagan

Dame Mary Fagan DCVO JP
Her Majesty's Lord-Lieutenant of Hampshire

ACKNOWLEDGEMENTS

THIS HISTORY IS the first published by the New Victoria County History of Hampshire volunteer project which aims to rewrite the Hampshire VCH volumes that were published a century ago. Few localities have changed more than the Basingstoke area, the first to be selected for study. Mapledurwell is the first parish to be published in the new VCH Hampshire series. It was chosen because of substantial research already carried out by Stan Waight on the estate there of Corpus Christi College, Oxford, and the good documentation available for the parish. Stan continues to research and write for the project. His research papers, which include the history of all the Corpus Christi College properties and copyholds in Mapledurwell, are deposited in Hampshire Record Office as the Waight papers (reference HRO, 83A02/10).

This book is very much a combined Hampshire effort. The main authors are John Hare, Michael Hicks, Jean Morrin and Stan Waight. Many others have contributed: John Chapman worked on the inclosure of 1797; Lorna Cuthill, Alan Hutton and Gordon Russell-Cave provided local information; Roger Ottewill researched and wrote the text on the Congregationalists; and Edward Roberts gave his expertise on the buildings. Wills and inventories relating to Mapledurwell were transcribed by the wills group which meets regularly in Basingstoke. Simon Townley and Mark Page of VCH Oxfordshire gave very valuable advice on research and writing. The task of integrating and editing the text fell to Jean Morrin and John Hare. The New VCH project has been guided from its inception by John Isherwood, who was then chairman of the Hampshire Archives Trust, and it is governed by the New VCH Partnership of that Trust, Hampshire Record Office on behalf of Hampshire County Council, the Hampshire Field Club and Archaeological Society, and the University of Winchester. It has been assisted at all stages by the Victoria County History, University of London, especially Professor John Beckett.

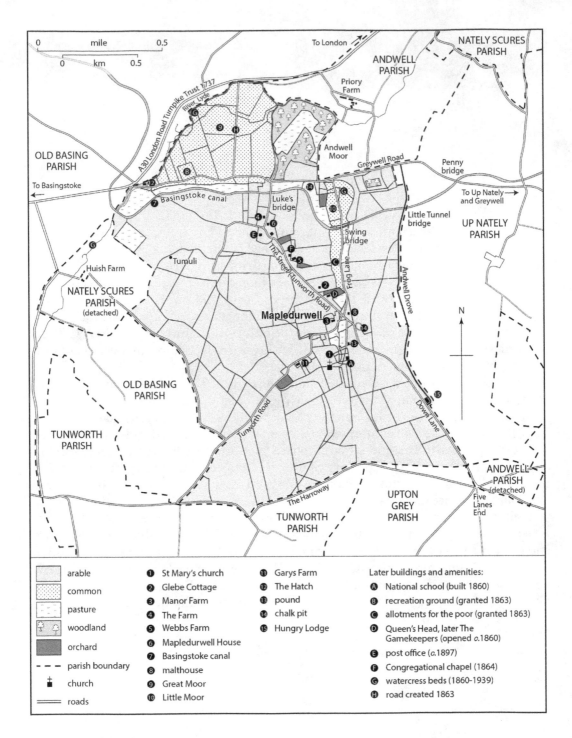

❶ St Mary's church
❷ Glebe Cottage
❸ Manor Farm
❹ The Farm
❺ Webbs Farm
❻ Mapledurwell House
❼ Basingstoke canal
❽ malthouse
❾ Great Moor
❿ Little Moor

⓫ Garys Farm
⓬ The Hatch
⓭ pound
⓮ chalk pit
⓯ Hungry Lodge

Later buildings and amenities:

Ⓐ National school (built 1860)
Ⓑ recreation ground (granted 1863)
Ⓒ allotments for the poor (granted 1863)
Ⓓ Queen's Head, later The Gamekeepers (opened c.1860)
Ⓔ post office (c.1897)
Ⓕ Congregational chapel (1864)
Ⓖ watercress beds (1860-1939)
Ⓗ road created 1863

Map 1   *Mapledurwell c. 1840.*

INTRODUCTION

THE RURAL PARISH of Mapledurwell is located on the north-eastern edge of the Hampshire downland, approximately 20 miles (32 km) to the north-east of Winchester and 3 miles (5 km) to the east of Basingstoke. In 1901 it covered 829 a. (335 ha.).[1] Although in many ways a deeply rural and slow-changing community, it has been dramatically affected by its proximity to the urban centre of Basingstoke. In the 15th and early 16th centuries, when Basingstoke and its hinterland became a major industrial and cloth producing area, it benefited both from the new markets and the industrial jobs. Investment occurred in the church and in housing, with the core of most of the older houses surviving from *c.* 1500–1650. Mapledurwell increased in wealth and size compared with many surrounding villages, and acquired a range of more specialised occupations. Since the late 20th century the sale of houses, construction of the motorway (M3), and the mechanisation of agriculture have transformed the village. The old houses remain but frequently with large additions and infill between them as the rural community has become a commuter village. Other changes would have happened without the influence of Basingstoke, such as the shift from the open common fields to separate fields due to inclosure in 1797, the growing concentration of land in fewer hands, and, in the 20th century, the mechanisation and consequent loss of agricultural labour.

In Domesday Book, Mapledurwell was one of a group of settlements that made up the larger manor of Mapledurwell. The manor was subsequently broken up, the central settlement providing an endowment for a religious house founded at Andwell and the eastern part of Newnham granted to another lord. After a period in lay hands, what was left of the original manor of Mapledurwell became in 1529 the possession of Corpus Christi College, Oxford, which remained the lord of the manor in 2012.[2] The adjacent priory of Andwell was also granted lands within Mapledurwell, but the priory lands were subsequently acquired by Bishop William of Wykeham for his new foundation of Winchester College.[3] Mapledurwell was a chapelry but it functioned as a parish and is treated as such in this text.

1   Census, 1901, Hampshire.
2   Corpus Christi College copyholds in Mapledurwell were numbered 2, 4–7, 9–11, 14–24. For the history of each see the Waight Papers, HRO 83A02/10. The numbers are those created for use in the college's accounts.
3   *VCH Hants*, II, 223–5. Winchester Coll. copyholds were numbered 1, 2, 5 and similarly were the numbers used by Winchester College.

Mapledurwell merged with neighbouring Up Nately and Andwell in 1932 to form a much larger civil parish.[4] The combined civil parish now comprises 2,121 acres (857 ha.).[5] Statistics after 1932 relate to the combined civil parish, so that after that date figures for the ancient parish of Mapledurwell are estimates. In ecclesiastical terms, Mapledurwell remained part of Newnham parish until 1922 and has subsequently been part of various ecclesiastical team ministries.

Parish Boundaries

Mapledurwell's original boundaries survived until the amalgamation with Up Nately in 1932. The parish is roughly rectangular and three of the four sections of boundary are still clearly defined by physical features. The northern boundary ran along the river Lyde which divides the Great Moor of Mapledurwell (inclosed 1863) from the parish of Old Basing to the north-west and the villages of Andwell and Up Nately to the north-east. The eastern boundary once divided the open fields of Mapledurwell from those of Up Nately and was defined by a track, now a public footpath, known as Andwell Drove. This track ran almost directly from north to south along the Up Nately side of the boundary to what is now known as Hungry Lodge. Whether it continued along the Up Nately

Figure 1 *The degraded bank and holloway on the southern boundary of the parish.*

4   Youngs, *Admin. Units*, Vol.1, 213; County of Southampton Review Order, 1932; *Kelly's Dir. Hants* (1935), 294.
5   http://www.visionofbritain.org.uk/unit_census_page.jsp?u_id=10180934&c_id=10001043. Accessed 30 November 2010.

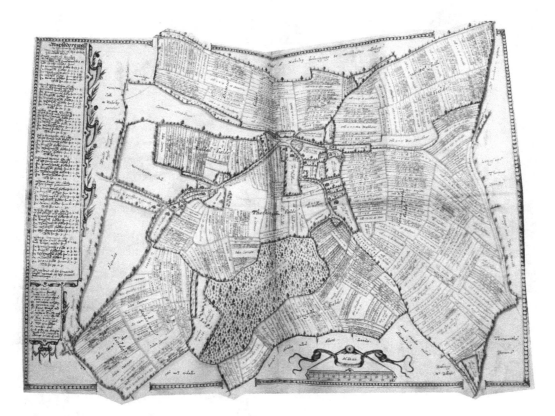

Map 2   *Langdon's map of Mapledurwell, 1616.*

side until the inclosure of Mapledurwell's common fields is not known, but the footpath
then linked with the upper part of Down Lane and runs south-east for 700 yards to
Five Lanes End. The Drove was not a long-distance route, but served merely to connect
the priory at Andwell with its detached land on the Up Nately down.[6] A bank (now
degraded) separated the two parishes. A rectangular inset into the boundary already
existed in 1616; it takes the form of a tree-lined inclosure of about 1.5 a. lying between
Mapledurwell's boundary and the Andwell Drove and was under cultivation in 1841.[7]
The southern boundary, which divides Mapledurwell from Upton Grey and Tunworth,
appears to have been of the double ditch form.[8] The western boundary divided the open
fields of Mapledurwell from those of Old Basing and was aligned generally with the
borders of their furlongs.[9] It is still marked by a degraded bank, by ancient hedgerows,
and in some places by lynchets that follow the curving pattern of the former strips and
furlongs.

6   OS Map 1:25000, sheet 144 (Explorer, 2005 edn).
7   HRO, 21M65/F239/1–2.
8   CCCO, Langdon Map MS 532/2/11; HRO, 10M57/P11; CCCO, Map 120.
9   CCCO, Langdon Map MS 532/2/11; HRO, 10M57/P11.

Figure 2 *A typical Mapledurwell landscape in 2012, looking south-west from The Gamekeepers pub.*

Figure 3 *A landscape, looking south-east from the church, 2012.*

Landscape

The parish may be divided into two parts. Most consists of undulating landscape, on the northern edge of Hampshire's chalk downland, with a topsoil of loam over a subsoil of chalk, and rising at the south-west boundary of the parish to about 110 m. Until inclosure in 1797, this area was covered by an extensive open field system (Map 2). The village was sited to profit from several springs and streams and its name, meaning maple tree spring, may have referred to a tree where the river Lyde rises.[10] Springs feed the stream which rises near the church and flows northward along Frog Lane, ultimately forming one tributary to the river Loddon. The clarity of its water is typical of chalkland streams and was suited to the cultivation of watercress, which accounted for much of the 9 a. of water in the parish in 1901. A large chalk pit, formerly used by all the parishioners, lies at the southern end of the village.[11]

A smaller and very different landscape area lies in the north of the parish bounded by the river Lyde: it consists of 84 a. of roughly level clay moorland lying at about 73 m. above sea level, and was traditionally used for grazing. The contrasts between the two landscapes are evident from Langdon's map (Map 2) and parts of the moor had been inclosed by 1615.

The landscape of the parish was also transformed in the later 18th century by the inclosure of the open fields in 1797, the construction of the Basingstoke canal just south of the moor in 1794, and by the grubbing up in the south-west of the parish of the Upgrove woodland from 1793[12] (Map 4). Inclosure of the northern moors occurred much later, the commons known as the Great and Little Moors being inclosed in 1863. Much more recently, in 1971, the landscape of the northern extremity of the parish was transformed by the construction of the M3 motorway which runs west to east through the Great Moor and has separated this part of the parish from the rest. It has also removed the peace and quiet of the northern end of the village.

Communications

A number of long distance routes pass through the parish. The ancient, possibly prehistoric, track across southern England known as the Harroway was called 'The Waye to London' in 1616, and ran along the headland inside the boundary of the southernmost open field of the village.[13] The line of the Roman road from Silchester to Chichester may be indicated by a ditch and early Roman sherd found to the east of The Hatch public house.[14] The main Basingstoke to London Road (now the A30) runs just outside the

---

10 R. Coates, *The Place-Names of Hampshire* (1989), 114. There are many varieties of spelling, especially Maplederwell (19th century), Mapledrewelle (11th century), Mapelth, Mapeth, Mapeldurewelle, Mapeldorwelle (12th century); Mapedrewell, Maperderewell, Mapeldereworth (13th century) and Mapuldurwell (15th century), see *VCH Hants*, IV, 149.
11 HRO, 21M65/F7/239/1.
12 HRO, Q23/2/81; CCCO, B/4/1/2, 61; CCCO, Map 120.
13 CCCO, Langdon Map MS 532/2/11.
14 HER 56603.

northern boundary of the parish and from 1737 formed part of the London to Salisbury turnpike road.[15]

In 1616 the only road access to the isolated village settlement was from the north, towards Basingstoke. A road branched east to Odiham from the Basingstoke to London road at Mapledurwell Hatch, and the village street (The Street) ran south-easterly from it to the centre of the village, and then south-west to Garys Farm where it ended (Map 1). Between 1616 and 1797 small lanes developed, one of which led from the southern end of The Street to Tunworth and the other from the village centre to Upton Grey. Those two lanes were upgraded to public carriageways by the inclosure award of 1797.[16] In 2012 the roads connecting Mapledurwell with the neighbouring villages of Basing, Up Nately, Upton Grey and Tunworth were still minor ones.

The parish was cut from east to west just south of the moor by the Basingstoke canal opened in 1794, but there was no wharf in Mapledurwell.[17] The construction of the canal was authorised in 1778 by a private Act of Parliament which gave Corpus Christi College specific authority for the sale of the land required.[18] There were numerous delays, particularly because of lack of investment, and construction did not begin until 1788 and it was never very profitable.[19] Tenants' land was divided by the construction and, although they were paid for it by the canal company, considerable resentment was provoked.[20] The four canal bridges within the parish were provided solely for local communications. The Mapledurwell section of the canal was almost totally derelict by 1964 because of the collapse of the tunnel in neighbouring Greywell in 1932;[21] its restoration was never attempted. Part of the canal on the Basingstoke side of where the Swing Bridge once stood was filled in by a local farmer, and the most westerly section between Luke's Bridge and The Hatch has been obliterated by the building of the M3 motorway in 1971 and consequent realignment of local roads.

15   10 Geo. 2 c.12, *Parl. Papers*, 1852, 1521 Turnpike Trusts, County Reports to the Secretary of State.
16   HRO, Q23/2/80.
17   P. A. L. Vine, *London's Lost Route to Basingstoke* (1968), 44–5.
18   CCCO, Cb 19/1.
19   Vine, *Lost Route to Basingstoke*, 44–5.
20   CCCO, F/3/3/7, pp.25, 89, 111. WC 23194. http://www.basingstoke-canal.org.uk/brlist.htm. Accessed 30 January 2011.
21   Basingstoke and Deane Borough Council, *Basingstoke Canal Conservation Area Appraisal* (April 2004).

SETTLEMENT AND POPULATION

MAPLEDURWELL IS A picturesque village with many attractive timber-framed houses and was designated a conservation area in 1981. There is considerable continuity in the pattern of roads and building from 1600 to the present, which may be attributed to the ownership of most of the parish by Corpus Christi College.[22]

Early Settlement

The earliest evidence for human activity in the parish is flintwork from the Palaeolithic period found on the slopes above the valley formed by the springs feeding the river Lyde.[23] That area continued to be attractive to early settlers in the following Mesolithic period, and evidence of Neolithic flint working suggests prehistoric industry.[24] Another prolific Mesolithic site was identified by fieldwalking on the slope of Nunnery Hill in the west of the parish; a rare broken macehead made from a quartzite river pebble was also found somewhere in that area.[25] Still visible in the landscape on the slopes east of the springs is a scheduled Bronze Age round barrow, and two ring ditches visible on aerial photographs are most probably ploughed out barrows.[26] A group of three barrows, two still present as low mounds and one identified from an aerial photograph, lies in the west of the parish in a field called Arborough Field.[27] The archaeological evaluation in 2004 prior to building east of The Hatch also discovered a large spread of burnt flint, possibly a levelled burnt mound, and a ditch dated by a Bronze Age bucket urn and struck flints.[28] Roman pottery has been found at several locations in the parish.[29]

Medieval and Later Settlement

The most useful pointer to the pattern of settlement lies in Langdon's detailed map of 1616 (Map 2). It shows the strips of the open fields, some small old inclosures, houses, and lanes, which, apart from the northern section of The Street, terminated at the

22 Basingstoke and Deane Borough Council, *Conservation Area Appraisal: Mapledurwell* (2001), 4.
23 HER 20428; OS ABRC SU65SE16.
24 HER 20429, 20383; OS ABRC SU65SE16; SU65SE16.
25 HER 32392, 20470; OS ABRC SU65SE74; SU65SE23. The significance of these is discussed by B. Cunliffe, 'Prehistoric and Roman North Hampshire' in Pevsner, *North Hampshire*, 8–13.
26 HER 20417; OS ABRC SU65SE17, 36060, 36061; HCC, 1984; Census AP, HCC, 1984.
27 HER 20414; 20415; 20416.
28 HER 56603.
29 HER 23048; 31244.

entrances to the common fields and pastures and made the area remote despite its
proximity to Basingstoke. The map and the present landscape suggest the presence of two
distinct settlements. The southern or lower one comprised the village centre and lay in a
sheltered hollow where The Street turns south-west near Manor Farm; it was central to
most of the open fields and it included on its fringes the parish church. That settlement is
now represented at the cross roads by Manor Farm, Manor Farm Cottage and barns, the
pond and in the south-westerly direction by the former copyholds of Arlings and Garys
Farm (Map 1).

A second and probably subsidiary settlement lay to the north of The Street, separated
from the lower village by the open fields and a stretch of The Street where it becomes a
holloway (Fig. 4). This upper settlement may have been associated with the expansion
of the open fields, and at its north end copyhold cottages began with The Farm and
extended southwards to the freehold Webbs Farmhouse. The gap between the two
settlements shows clearly on the 1616 and 1797 maps, with Thatchingham and Musdale
fields stretching down to the road and with no sign of any desertion of tenements (Map
1). Most (15) of the Corpus Christi College copyhold cottages, of which ten survive
in 2012, lay in those two settlements at either end of The Street. Most of the surviving
cottages date from late 16th century or later, although a few earlier houses and farms
survive, the earliest example being Rye Cottage, dated by dendrochronology to 1487
(Fig. 5).[30]

Figure 4 *The Street, looking south and showing its character as a holloway which had open fields on
either side.*

30   HER 2361; E. Roberts, *Hampshire Houses, 1250–1700* (2003), 22.

Infill was already occurring in the 19th century. New tenements were created. In 1802 Mapledurwell House was built opposite The Farm at the north end of The Street. The Gamekeepers public house was built *c.* 1860 on the east side of The Street just north of the village crossroads. But there were also losses as in July 1881 when a disastrous fire erupted near the village crossroads, destroying the whole of Corpus Christi College copyhold 6. The fire spread northwards across the road, damaging the farm buildings of Manor Farm, although the house itself survived.[31] Two adjoining houses of agricultural workers were destroyed and were apparently never rebuilt. The substantial house leased by Joseph Addison, the freeholder, was also destroyed although the adjoining cottage, occupied by the widow Hockley, which was part of the same leasehold, survived and is now known as Manor Farm Cottage (Fig. 9).[32] In 2012 mainly modern infill gives the sense of almost continuous development from the north of The Street south to Garys farmhouse, where large, recently-constructed barns fronting the east side of The Street somewhat conceal the pattern of earlier settlement (Fig. 11). The Street remains a very narrow winding lane, designated unsuitable for heavy goods vehicles. The minor village street, Frog Lane, runs in a north-easterly direction from the cross roads. There was very little early settlement on Frog Lane, apart from the malthouse on Winchester College land at its far south-eastern end. Frog Lane follows the stream where watercress beds were developed during the 19th century; at its northern end there is some modern development.

The whole village retains a rural atmosphere with well-spaced buildings, although there has been much enlargement of the original houses within the individual tenements. The lack of development is due, at least in part, to the 1933 agreement between Corpus Christi College and Basingstoke RDC that land in the parish should be designated as open spaces or restricted to agricultural, horticultural and silvicultural use.[33] However, the village was increasingly run down in the late 19th and early 20th century, and by the early 1950s many farm workers' cottages were empty. In 1964 a change in the law allowed Corpus Christi College to sell them.[34] This facilitated gentrification, especially as cottage sales by the college coincided with the development of Basingstoke as a London overspill town, the expansion of the defence industry in the local area at the Atomic Weapons Research Establishment (now AWE) Aldermaston and at Farnborough, and the growth in commuting to London. In 2012 most residents commuted to Basingstoke or London.

Apart from infill and the enlargement of existing houses in The Street, new development has been largely confined to the north of the parish. A village hall with associated leisure facilities opened in the 1970s just south of the motorway. In the 21st century some 20 houses have been built near the canal and just east of Frog Lane. The biggest development has been east of The Hatch public house along the main road (A30) where an industrial estate with 11 units and 60 flats offering social and affordable housing was constructed in the first decade of the 21st century.

31   *Hants and Berks Gazette*, 9 July 1881. Charred timbers were uncovered during alterations in 2007; information from the owner
32   CCCO, CH10.
33   CCCO, LB 42/101.
34   Universities and Colleges Estates Act 1964, *c.* 51.

Figure 5 *Rye Cottage, constructed with crucks c. 1487 and given a box-framed extension in 1526.*

Figure 6 *Island Cottages, a group of 19th-century cottages in Kembers Lane.*

Figure 7 *Jasmine Cottage.*

SECULAR BUILDINGS

Fifteen of the structures standing in the parish before 1932 survive in 2012 and are included on the National Heritage Register: St Mary's church, 11 houses, The Hatch public house, a canal bridge, and a cart-shed.[35] Except for the church, which is of national importance, all are listed because of their local or regional special interest. All the houses can be identified with specific tenancies, copyhold and freehold, of the manors of Andwell and Mapledurwell. Apart from Mapledurwell House, all are of timber-framed construction, although some have brick infill or façades applied subsequently. The majority have a core that goes back to the 16th and early 17th century. Using Langdon's 1616 map and the court records, six of them — Arlings, Manor Farm, now called Manor Farmhouse (Fig. 8), Maple Cottage, Mittens, Rose Cottage, and Rye Cottage (Fig. 5) — can be identified with Corpus Christi College manorial copyholds, Webbs Farmhouse was part of a manorial freehold and the remaining four — Addison's Farm House, Ivy House (formerly Ivy Cottage), Jasmine Cottage (Fig. 7) and Mapledurwell House (Fig. 10) — were built on Winchester College land. The Hatch public house was built

---

35   This section owes a great deal to the expertise of Edward Roberts. National Heritage Register numbers 1092946–50, 1092979, 1179164, 1179175, 1179183, 1179209, 1302062, 1302128, 1339513–4, 1339551 (http://www.english-heritage.org.uk/professional/protection/process/national-heritage-list-for-england. Accessed 14 July 2012).

on a copyhold that had apparently been created from the Great Moor in 1729.[36] The old houses were spread out along The Street, and given the size of their plots all would have had ample space for a small farmyard. Only one working farm, named Garys after its 19th-century occupiers, remains and the rest of the old houses are now in private, domestic use.

Building before 1700

The majority of the listed buildings have a timber-framed core belonging to the 16th and early 17th century, though elements in Maple Cottage and Garys Farmhouse could well date to any time in the late 15th century and details in Mittens could be of *c.* 1500. Otherwise, the earliest house is Rye Cottage, a three-bay cruck cottage dated by dendrochronology to 1487, which has a one-bay box-framed extension of 1525–6.[37] Most of the others were built before 1650. Such a widespread rebuilding of so many of the village houses from the late 15th to the 17th century suggests considerable prosperity in the village at that time. Subsequent alterations generally consisted of brick infilling, added façades, or additions to the timber-framed core. The timber-framed houses are

Figure 8 *Manor Farmhouse.*

36   CCCO, F/3/3/4, p.214. The transaction was for three new lives, suggesting that the copyhold was created then. It is not shown on Langdon's map and probably was taken in from the Great Moor.

37   Roberts, *Hampshire Houses*, 236–7.

generally of rectangular plan, some of the roofs half-hipped, some gable-ended, some thatched, and some tiled. At least three houses appear to have had cross wings added at some stage, in particular Manor Farmhouse which was the principal messuage of the largest copyhold.

The dwellings are of the type that has been described as 'rural vernacular houses',[38] although it is clear from the quality of the buildings that agriculture in Mapledurwell was a source of considerable wealth for the tenants at the time of their construction and that some must have been built as the messuages of 'standard' eight-acre copyholds.[39]

Building from 1700 to 1900

Few surviving buildings appear to have been started during the period. The house now known as Manor Farm Cottage (Fig. 9) has a brick façade apparently of high quality belying the interior, which contains two bays of much-altered timber framing and may have had another half-bay at the southern end. The interior's flimsy timber with much crude joinery suggests a late date, possibly in the early 18th century. The brick skin was added in two phases, and the chimney is also an added feature. The whole was a plan like an agricultural building with a loft for hay or malt.[40] Tenants' wills of 1645 and 1693 mention a malthouse or brewhouse on the site,[41] and a court book entry justified a reduced renewal fine in 1714 by saying that the copyholder Henry Smith was 'kindly used in consideration of his house being burnt'.[42] Perhaps the Smith family carried out at least a partial conversion of the malthouse for domestic use about that time, resulting in the present cottage.[43] A new principal messuage, built on the site of the old one, was destroyed in the fire of 1881 when it was on lease at rack-rent to Joseph Addison.[44] In 1802 Mapledurwell House, a new gentry residence, was built.[45]

No further domestic building appears to have taken place in the village until the second half of the 19th century when The Gamekeepers public house and four cottages were built on land which had once been William Bundy's copyhold in Frog Lane.[46] The cottages were for farm employees: rectangular, gable-ended, rendered, tile-roofed and simple in style.[47] The college also built another and similar group of four cottages in Kembers Lane, now Island Cottages (Fig. 6), between acquiring the freehold in 1864 and the cottagers paying rent in 1869.[48] Since 1964 and the sale of college cottages there has been considerable expansion of existing houses, and the infill of new housing.

38   *ibid.*, 216–7.
39   *ibid.*, 217.
40   Elizabeth Lewis and Edward Roberts, personal comment.
41   HRO, 1645A/47; 1693AD/105.
42   CCCO, F/3/3/4, 137.
43   On the Smiths, see below, Economic History and Tenant Farming, 1640–1800.
44   CCCO, F/1/1/2.
45   Below, The Major Freeholder and Fig. 10.
46   HRO, Q23/2/81.
47   CCCO, F/1/4/1.
48   CCCO, LB 38/367; F/1/4/1.

Figure 9 *Manor Farm Cottage, with a brick front added to earlier buildings.*

Population

We lack figures for medieval population. Domesday Book lists a total of 26 families or tenants, but this covers a large complex manor that included the later Mapledurwell, Up Nately, Andwell, and Newnham. In the early 14th century, in 1327 and 1334, Mapledurwell was one of the smaller and poorer parishes of Basingstoke hundred. In 1327 eight men were taxed, although this cannot be taken as a complete list of families present in the village.[49] During the later Middle Ages, Mapledurwell grew in wealth, size and position compared with most villages in the area. By 1525 there were 35 households and the village had risen to become the fourth most populous one in Basingstoke hundred.[50] There then seems to have followed a period of continuity, at least in terms of the number of households, until the 19th century. Twenty-one houses were assessed for the hearth tax in 1665.[51] Fifteen were not chargeable making a total of 36 households, and in 1811 there were 40 families in 35 houses.[52] In the 19th century the population increased steadily from 160 in 1801, 172 in 1811, 190 in 1831 to 237 in 1881 when 57 houses were occupied, but fell to 207 in 49 houses in 1891. This was despite the fact that

49   TNA, E 179/173/4 (HRO microfilm 362a); P. Mitchell-Fox and M. Page (eds), *The Hampshire Tax List of 1327* (H.R.S., forthcoming).
50   TNA, E 179/183.
51   *Hearth Tax*, 236.
52   HRO, 49M67/P02.

the numbers given for 1891 were for the civil parish to which parts of Nately Scures had been added.[53] The significant drop in the number of houses between 1881 and 1891 may be explained by the disastrous fire of July 1881.[54] Population then rose to 221 in 1911.[55]

Immigration was small-scale and local with incomers arriving in the 18th century from the surrounding parishes of Basing, Tunworth, Andwell, North Waltham, Weston Patrick, and Nately Scures.[56] Similarly, in the mid to late 19th century the majority of villagers were born in the parish (63 per cent), with others mainly coming from the surrounding rural parishes (31 per cent). In 1861 only 6 per cent of residents were born outside Hampshire in Berkshire (3), Essex (2), Kent (2), London (2), Surrey (2) with one each from Staffordshire, Sussex and Wiltshire. One incoming family were the Dudneys, listed as market gardeners from 1871–81, who came from Sussex with children born in Kent. In 1891 one agricultural labourer born in the neighbouring parish of Upton Grey had a wife and three children born in East India. Population mobility increased until in 1901 only 30 per cent of the residents were born in Mapledurwell and 18 per cent of the population of 202 were born outside Hampshire, mainly in London (8) and the home counties, especially neighbouring Berkshire (13). But even in 1901 more than 75 per cent of the population were born in the local area.[57]

The population was relatively stable until 1961 when the population of the parish was estimated at 220.[58] In 2001 the population of the combined parish was 446 in 168 households suggesting a population of about 300 in Mapledurwell, and this has since increased with new housing built in the north of the village.

LANDOWNERSHIP

Mapledurwell was already separate from Basing in 1065 and was under the feudal system held from 1086 of the king in chief for service of half a knight's fee.[59] The manor preceded the fully-formed parish structure and was larger than the modern parish. The sub-manors of Andwell in the early 12th century and Newnham in 1198 were carved out of it. Mapledurwell manor retained some holdings in Up Nately and Newnham in and after 1535,[60] and freehold and copyhold tenancies in the neighbouring parishes of Nately Scures, Newnham, and Up Nately. The manor of Mapledurwell descended in the Port family until confiscated in 1172 and was granted to Bassets, from whom it descended to the Bassets, Despensers, Beauchamps and their coheirs, the last of whom, George Lord Abergavenny, sold it in 1513 to William Frost, who later conveyed it to Corpus

53   TNA, ED 21/ 6498.
54   Above, Settlement.
55   TNA RG14/6285.
56   HRO, 49M67/PW1. 18th century list of 'certificates and bonds brought to Mapledurwell'.
57   Census, 1851–1901.
58   TNA, RG 13/1109/35–38; www.visionofbritain.org.uk/census. Accessed 30 November 2010, Mapledurwell CP/Ch, Population and Housing, Table Views. The census figures rise sharply reflecting the addition of Up Nately in 1932. There were 99 houses by 1951 and 344 inhabitants, but 188 houses in 1961 and only 322 residents.
59   *Inq.p.m*, I, 807; IX, 428.
60   *VCH Hants*, IV, 151; *Valor Eccl.*,II, 246.

Christi College, Oxford. It remained in the hands of the college from 1529 to the present day. Since the lords were all of national importance, Mapledurwell shared in a series of national upheavals, being devastated in 1234 and 1321, and forfeited in 1322, 1400, 1459, and 1471, albeit temporarily.

Mapledurwell Manor

Mapledurwell was held by Anschetill in 1065 and in 1086 by Hubert de Port,[61] presumably a brother or other kinsman of Hugh de Port, lord of Basing, formerly of St Jean le Thomas in western Normandy. The Mapledurwell branch of the de Ports held lands in other counties, collectively called the honour of Kington in 1166.[62] Adam de Port founded Andwell Priory and endowed it with land carved out of Mapledurwell now in Up Nately.[63] It descended to his grandson, also Adam de Port, who in 1172 was outlawed for treason and forfeited all his possessions.[64]

The Basset Descent

Richard I granted Mapledurwell with Woking (Surr.) to Alan Basset (d. 1232) for one knight's fee,[65] and the manor descended among his descendants until 1513. In 1198 Alan had granted three hides in Newnham, part of Mapledurwell, to Hugh de Arundel to hold to him and his heirs for the service of half a knight's fee, thus completing the division of the Domesday manor into three separate manors.[66] To end his disputes with the monks of Andwell in 1223 he restored to them 'a way sufficient for a horse laden to go along with his leader in the head of his tillage toward the water of Maplederwell to the house of Endewelle', obtaining in return a release of their claim in Hook wood and 'land in the field "*del su*" of the chapel of Mapeldurwelle'.[67] Because Alan's son Gilbert (d. 1241)[68] sided against Henry III's alien counsellors, his wood of Mapledurwell was broken by royal command, timber was carried away and houses razed to the ground. Reparation was made in 1234, when Gilbert was authorised to re-inclose his wood, recover his timber and rebuild his premises.[69] In 1280 Mapledurwell manorial court punished infringements against the assize of bread and ale which regulated the sale of these vital products.[70]

61   *VCH Hants*, I, 487*a*.
62   *Gen.* NS, XVI, 9–12.
63   *VCH Hants*, II, 223; WCM 2788.
64   *Archaeol. Jnl*, IX, 249; *Pipe R. 13 Hen. II* (PRS), p.189; *Gen.* NS, XVI, 10.
65   *Red Book Exch.*, I, 198.
66   Feet of F. Hants, East. 9 Ric. I; *Pipe Roll 9 Ric. I* (PRS 23), no.152; *Basset Charters* (PRS ns 50), no. 81.
67   *Basset Charters*, no. 211.
68   *Excerpta e Rot. Fin.* (Rec. Com.) I, 231; *Testa de Nevill* (Rec. Com.), 238*b*.
69   *Cal. Close*, 1227–34, 441, 495.
70   *Plac. de Quo Warr.*, 770, 772. See also *Hund. R.* (Rec. Com.), II, 221.

The Despenser Descent Onward

From the Basset heiress, Alina countess of Norfolk (d. 1306), the manor descended to her son Hugh Despenser the elder,[71] Edward II's favourite and earl of Winchester from 1322, who in 1318 obtained a grant of free warren, minor hunting rights, in his demesne lands of Mapledurwell.[72] Following Despenser's exile and forfeiture in 1321, his enemies entered Mapledurwell and other of his manors and committed various offences there.[73] Subsequently recalled, he was hanged by the forces of Queen Isabella outside Bristol on 27 October 1326, his son Hugh the younger suffering a month later at Hereford. Although initially confiscated and granted out by Edward III, Mapledurwell was fully restored in 1337 to a third Hugh Despenser, son of Hugh Despenser the younger, whence it descended to his great-nephew Thomas, favourite of Richard II and briefly earl of Gloucester, who perished in 1400 with the Ricardian earls in rebellion against Henry IV. Although initially confiscated, Mapledurwell was restored to Thomas' son Richard Lord Despenser, who died under-age in 1414,[74] and passed to his sister Isabel countess of Warwick and Worcester (d. 1439), then to her son and her grand-daughter Anne Beauchamp (d. 1449). Although disputed between the issue of Isabel's two marriages, Mapledurwell was secured by her youngest daughter Anne Beauchamp, wife of Richard Neville the powerful earl of Warwick (later called the 'kingmaker'), and then by Richard duke of Gloucester (the future Richard III) in right of her daughter and his consort Anne Neville.[75] It was probably as king that Richard III conceded Mapledurwell to George Lord Abergavenny (d. 1492), the other coheir.[76] Described as the manor and four farmsteads 100 a., 30 a. meadow, 100 a. pasture, 100 a. wood, 60 s. rent in Mapledurwell, Eastrop, Up Nately, and Newnham, it was sold in 1513 by George's son (also George Lord Abergavenny) to William Frost, steward of Richard Fox, Bishop of Winchester, founder of Corpus Christi College, Oxford, and a prominent member of the local gentry.[77] Frost settled Mapledurwell on Corpus Christi College 'for the support to the end of time of a fellow of his own blood',[78] which took full effect on Frost's death in 1529. Corpus Christi College still held the manor in 2012.[79]

The Priory of Andwell and Winchester College

Mapledurwell also included land belonging to the neighbouring manor of Andwell. The de Ports, who had held the large Domesday manor of Mapledurwell, had founded a monastery at Andwell. They endowed it with lands in the central part of the manor, in what became known as Up Nately, but also included some land in the western part

71 *Feudal Aids*, II, 313.
72 *Cal. Chart.* 1300–26, 382; *Cal. Close* 1318–23, 543.
73 *Cal. Pat.* 1321–4, 165.
74 *Cal. Pat.* 1399–1401, 417; *Cal. Inq. Misc. VII*, nos. 3, 182, 479.
75 TNA, DL 26/69.
76 In a January before October 1485, CCCO, 6 Cap 13 (1), 4; TT, 203–4.
77 CCCO, 6 Cap 13 (1), 13, 14, 16, 17; TNA CP 40/998 carte Hil. 4 Hen. VIII, m. 1d.
78 CCCO, 6 Cap 13 (2), 23; TT 11, 13, 27.
79 Personal communication from CCCO estates Bursar.

of what remained as Mapledurwell. The priory belonged to the abbey of Tiron in France who later sold it in 1391 to William of Wykeham, who used it to endow his new foundation of Winchester College (Map 3). The manor of Andwell remained in the hands of the latter until the present.[80]

The Major Freeholder[81]

The Canners were a local farming family from 1450 to 1641.[82] In 1487, when there were seven freehold tenancies, including a mill of Merton priory and a tenement and 8 a. of Monk Sherborne priory, John Canner held the largest freehold; a messuage and 60 a., held for fealty, suit of court and 7s. rent. The family was a prominent one in Mapledurwell from the beginning of the 15th century as well as in Basingstoke, and its members were among the most highly assessed villagers in 1525.[83] The main estate remained intact in Canner hands until the death on 1641 of the last John Canner,[84] when the property passed to Thomas Kent and in c. 1652 to John Sumner.[85] Another John Sumner was proprietor in 1895.[86] The original house was replaced in 1802 by a substantial gentry building, Mapledurwell House, constructed on a freehold Winchester College plot (Fig. 10). Thomas Page, the owner in 1815, described himself as gentleman of Mapledurwell, and his choice of executors, the rector of the neighbouring parish of Tunworth and a Basingstoke surgeon, suggests he was a part of the local genteel society.[87] Page and his gentry successors in Mapledurwell House were distinct socially from much of the farming community, though in the 20th century they played an active role in the village.[88] Joseph Addison, for example, was born in Wenham Hall, Essex[89] and was described as a landed proprietor in 1861 when he was living with his family, a coachman, cook and housemaid in Mapledurwell House; in 1871 he was a medical professional, though not practising, and farmed 105 acres. His six-bedroom house, with coach house, stable, many other outhouses, lawn and pleasure grounds, was valued in total at £830 even though some of the pleasure grounds belonged to Winchester College and the undefined nature of the boundary between the two 'was of great detriment to the sale value of the property'.[90] Addison's cellar contained 42 bottles of champagne including Moët & Chandon, sherry, claret, brandy, and port of which 12 bottles had been laid down

80   *VCH Hants*, 2, 1903, 223.
81   CCCO, C6 10/1.
82   CCCO, Cb 1/2.
83   For the Canner family, see below, Social History.
84   HRO, 1641A/10.
85   CCCO, a 1/4; F 3/3/1, 35.
86   Winchester City Library, H33/3f.
87   TNA, PROB 11/1572.
88   Below, Social History.
89   TNA, RG 9/709.
90   TNA RG 10/1235. Stated by James Harris, valuer: HRO, 50M/63/B1/32.

Figure 10 *Mapledurwell House, a substantial gentry house.*

in 1847.[91] Between 1923 and 1948, the house was occupied by a series of senior army officers, namely Brig. Gen. Stopford, Col. Goring and Lt. Col. Hamilton.[92]

Other Freeholders

In 1839 James Webb held Webbs Farmhouse, other property and 58 a.[93] This had been purchased by Corpus Christi College from the estate of Edward Covey of Basingstoke for £3,218 in September 1864,[94] and was then united with the Manor Farm. Webbs Farmhouse was sold by the college in March 1971.[95]

LOCAL GOVERNMENT

In the Middle Ages, local government was effectively the work of the manor courts at Mapledurwell and the hundred court of Basingstoke, the latter representing a unit of the

91   HRO, 50M63/B1/31.
92   *Kelly's Dirs. Hampshire, Wiltshire, and Dorset, 1923–48, passim.*
93   HRO, 21 M65/F7/152/1–2.
94   CCCO, LB 38/367.
95   CCCO, LB 53/4.

county, in this case Basingstoke and its surrounding villages. The responsibility for the maintenance of peace was carried out through the community or tithings, into which all males over the age of twelve had to be enrolled, and whose chosen tithingman had to report infringements of the peace to the hundred court at the view of frankpledge[96] in the courts of Mapledurwell and of Basingstoke. Meanwhile, the lord maintained his rights as landlord through the court of Mapledurwell itself.

Mapledurwell tenants thus owed suit, or responsibility, both to the hundred court of Basingstoke and to the court of Mapledurwell. In 1274, the lord of the manor, Ela, countess of Warwick, widow of Philip Basset, was already exercising part of the jurisdiction of the hundred court by holding her own assize of bread and ale at Mapledurwell, regulating the sale of these two vital products, and by not allowing her manorial tenants or villeins to perform suit of court at Basingstoke in 1274, when she was required to explain by what right she did this.[97] Later Mapledurwell tenants were still responsible to the court of Basingstoke hundred, as in 1399 when William Badekoc and William Canner were fined for fighting and breaking the peace, or in 1464 when fines were issued to John Coudray for allowing a felled tree to block the highway, and to John atte Fielde, the earl of Warwick's bailiff, for impounding in Mapledurwell oxen, cows, and calves belonging to John Stukeley, the lord of nearby Newnham.[98] In the last case, there seems to have been a conflict between the hundred and local jurisdictions: John atte Fielde justified his action because Stukeley owed 6s. 8d. to Richard Neville, earl of Warwick, the lord of Mapledurwell, for fines in the latter's court there.[99] The activity of the Mapledurwell court is shown in the few surviving court rolls, of 1450, 1512 and 1516, which all described the courts as view of frankpledge and show them presenting a full range of accusations.[100] The court then clearly operated the assize of ale, and also fined the miller of Andwell for taking excessive toll, or charges.[101] Furthermore, Mapledurwell did not pay cert money to the Basingstoke court, a payment required by the hundred court from many of the other villages.[102] Manorial courts offered opportunities for the village elite to influence local affairs through their role among the 12 free jurors as elected officials of the manor or representatives of the community, as assessors, or as a tithingman. In the manor court, new tenants came and formally acquired land from the lord, the court rolls providing the official record of the land transfer whether of land in the village itself or of neighbouring land belonging to the lord of the manor (for example, in 1450 a virgate, about 30 a. of land, in Eastrop was taken by a man from Nately). The courts also influenced aspects of the local economy through dealing with stray animals, particularly sheep, pannage of the pigs (rent for their feeding), or overburdening of pasture.

---

96   By which tenants were held mutually responsible within a group of ten households.
97   Baigent and Millard, *Basingstoke*, 181,188, 238, 241.
98   Baigent and Millard, *Basingstoke*, 241, 247, 258, 293.
99   Baigent and Millard, *Basingstoke*, 293–4.
100 Three court rolls were examined (CCCO, Cb/1/2 (1450); 1/4 (1512); 1/5 (1516)); a few additional rolls were unfit for examination.
101 Mapledurwell does not seem to have possessed a mill, but fines were regularly levied. In 1516 the miller is specified as 'of Andwell'
102 Baigent and Millard, *Basingstoke*, 238.

The Manorial Courts, 1500–1700

After the acquisition of the manor by Corpus Christi College in 1529, most of the parish's tenants had to attend its manor court. During the 16th and 17th centuries the college held a court baron and court leet (view of frankpledge) in Mapledurwell on the same day.

The court baron managed Corpus Christi College's copyhold estate in Mapledurwell, Up Nately and Newnham, whereas the court leet mainly regulated agricultural practice within Mapledurwell parish and elected the hayward to control stray cattle, and tithing men who maintained law and order, from among the freeholders and copyholders.[103] Decisions of the court baron could be disputed, as in 1553–5 when the college upheld the rights in reversion of Richard Smith, on his late father's copyhold, to inherit rather than Joan, his stepmother, who claimed widow's rights in Chancery as the second wife, widow and executrix, to whom Thomas Smith had left all his goods with the exception of a few small specified gifts (Richard was left one sheep only).[104] In 1663 freeholders from Holdshot, Eastrop, and Headley, and copyholders in Up Nately and Newnham as well as Mapledurwell owed homage to the lord of the manor.[105]

Some court rolls from 1529 to 1694 survive at Corpus Christi College, and court books from the mid 17th to mid 19th century. Rolls survive only sporadically from the early 16th century. Courts were held once a year in most years from 1580 to 1640, though from 1640 to 1660 apparently only five courts were held.[106] There may have been disruption as a result of the Parliamentarian sieges of Basing House in the adjoining parish of Old Basing; the name Hungry Lodge in the south-east of the parish is said to have originated when Roundhead troops reputedly called there demanding food.[107] Courts were held annually or biannually after 1660, with those immediately after the Restoration thoroughly reviewing and regulating agricultural practice.[108]

Until the end of the 17th century the representatives of the lord of the manor stayed at Manor Farm and presumably held the court there.[109] By 1793 the officials were staying at The Hatch public house where the court may also have been held.[110] The receipts of the courts from renewal fines and amercements (discretionary fines) ranged in value from as much £174 in 1666, when the major copyholds of Mapledurwell and Newnham were renewed together with many fines or amercements, to only £1 the following year.[111]

The court leet regulated the use of the commons including stints, the common fields, watercourses, boundaries, the pound, the stocks and the butts, as well as policing encroachments.[112] The accusation against Roger Smith in 1660 of taking soil from the commons to his Winchester College land illustrated the problem arising from some

103 CCCO, F/3/3/3, 125.
104 TNA, C1/1383/27–29; CCCO, CH 4; HRO, 1552U/59.
105 CCCO, Ca1/5.
106 CCCO, F/3/3/1.
107 *Hampshire Treasures*, 2, 182
108 For example CCCO F/3/3/3, 4; Ca 1/5 1663.
109 CCCO, Newlyn letter no.21, 25 May 1691.
110 CCCO, Cb 18/10.
111 CCCO, Cb 4/27.
112 CCCO, Ma 2/11; Cb 4/7; Cb 4/34; F/3/3/3, 58 & 233; F/3/3/4, 181, 196, 220.

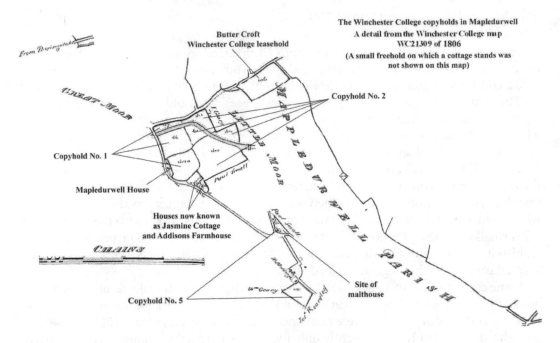

Map 3   *Land in Mapledurwell belonging to the manor of Andwell.*

tenants owning land in both manors.[113] In 1670 he was fined again for ploughing up a ley bank and joining his Corpus Christi and Winchester College lands.[114] Civil offences were also punished, such as that of Widow Knight who was presented for selling ale without licence and keeping 'ill orders on the Sabbath'.[115]

Apart from the manorial officials, Corpus Christi College appointed a local bailiff for day-to-day management of their Mapledurwell and other Hampshire estates. He collected rents and fines, awarded trees for repairs, and collected the heriot on the death of a tenant, although in 1693 after Henry Smith died of smallpox, the bailiff was forbidden by his family to collect the heriot.[116] The bailiff could not seal copyholds. The bailiff's role increased and the regulatory role of the manorial court declined in the 18th and 19th centuries, until in 1819 the rector warned the college bursar that only one old man knew anything about the boundaries of the manor.[117]

Courts baron continued to be held about every three years in the late 18th and early 19th centuries. Their infrequency caused discontent among new copyholders who wanted to register their interests.[118] The court baron ceased in 1850, by which time many

113   CCCO, F/3/3/3.
114   CCCO, F/3/3/3, 107.
115   CCCO, F/3/3/3, 125
116   CCCO, Newlyn letter no.26, 12 May 1692.
117   CCCO, Cb 16/11.
118   CCCO, F/3/3/9, 309; Cb 18/4, 18/10.

copyholds had already been extinguished or amalgamated. The few that remained were regulated directly from Corpus Christi College in Oxford.[119]

Parish Government and Officers

Although Mapledurwell was a chapelry of Newnham until 1922, it operated in many ways as a separate parish with its own parish registers, churchwardens and overseers of the poor. Churchwardens' accounts exist from 1616 and some overseers' accounts survive from 1690. Parish officials from the 17th century increasingly replaced the court leet in regulating village life. In the 17th and 18th centuries, two churchwardens and two overseers were appointed annually, chosen from the leading copyholders and freeholders. There are references to the office of constable from 1634, for which office Mr Gary was paid £1 16s. in 1783 and to a surveyor of highways from 1691.[120] One churchwarden was appointed by the rector, the other was chosen by the parish. The churchwardens cared for the church and paid those in receipt of passing charity, such as maimed soldiers and poor Irish in 1634. In the second half of the 17th century a few women held office: Widow Matthew succeeded Henry Ifould as co-churchwarden in 1665, when William Ayres, her bailiff, was allowed to act for her. In 1693 Widow Matthew was appointed senior overseer. Widow Sumner presented accounts on behalf of her late husband as churchwarden in 1675.[121] Overseers' accounts survive from 1690–1778 and from 1783–1829.[122] The accounts for the 18th century show the parish rate paying for some fuel, shoes and spinning, but by 1770 the parish rate was used mainly to give weekly cash payments to the poor with occasional payments for rent. Itemised accounts begin in 1758–9 and included money paid to the county, for example of £3 8s. 8d. in 1761–2.[123]

Mapledurwell civil parish was established under the Local Government Act of 1894 with the same boundaries as the ecclesiastical parish. There was one parish meeting a year from 1894–1922 and two from 1923–31.[124] The vestry continued to run the parish assisted by churchwardens, overseers of the poor and two allotment wardens who were responsible for the allotments and leisure grounds given to the inhabitants under the inclosure of 1863.[125] In 1922 the vestry was replaced by the parochial church council, following the creation of the separate curacy. The gentry of Mapledurwell House played an increasing role in local affairs in the 20th century when the owner was usually appointed rector's churchwarden.[126]

In 1932, Mapledurwell was amalgamated with the neighbouring parish of Up Nately and Andwell, to form Mapledurwell and Up Nately parish council;[127] a new parish

---

119 See for example, CCCO, LB 41/323.
120 HRO, 49M67/PR1, PO2.
121 HRO, 49M67/PR1.
122 HRO, 49M67, PO1–2.
123 HRO, 49M67, PO1.
124 Parish council minutes 1894–1931, held by clerk to parish in 2012.
125 HRO, 49M67/PV1, 49M67/P22.
126 HRO, 49M67/ PP1.
127 Youngs, *Admin. Units*, Vol. 1, 213: formed under the County of Southampton Review Order, 1932; *Kelly's Dir. Basingstoke* (1935), 294.

council was formed in February that year.[128] The civil parish was within Basingstoke RDC. Under local government reorganization in 1974 Mapledurwell and Up Nately civil parish became part of Basingstoke and Deane District Council. In 2010, Mapledurwell and Up Nately parish council comprised five members with a clerk, who met six times a year and reported annually to the parish assembly on local planning, environmental and leisure issues.[129]

128 Parish council minutes were held by clerk of the parish in 2010.
129 http://www.mapledurwell.gov.uk. Accessed 30 May 2011.

Mapledurwell is an agricultural parish although few now work the land. Agriculture was mixed in character with sheep being the main livestock. Until the mid 19th century the village centre was inhabited by yeomen and husbandmen who were mainly customary tenants or copyholders, except for a few freeholders, of whom only one had a substantial holding, and one leaseholder. In 1616 seven arable open fields surrounded the village together with 100 a. (40 ha.) of moorland in the far north and 40 a. (16 ha.) of woodland; the fields were inclosed in 1797 and the moor in 1863. A variety of rural trades and crafts were practised and a malt industry developed from between the 17th and 19th centuries.

THE AGRICULTURAL LANDSCAPE

Langdon's magnificent map of Mapledurwell in 1616 (Map 2) provides a clear image of agriculture as it had been practised in the locality since the Middle Ages. The map shows that the parish, with the exception of a small area of woodland and the northern stretch of open moorland pasture adjoining the river Lyde, was covered by open strip fields typical of the chalklands. Although there was no sign of any extensive downland permanent sheep pasture, nevertheless substantial flocks could still have been maintained since the manor then used a two-field rotation with half the land being maintained as fallow, as in 1381.[130] Before 1616 parts of the arable may have been specialist downland pasture, as reflected in the field names of Downfield and White Hill Field (Map 5). By 1616, there was a more intensive rotation and the extent of the cultivated area had also reached a peak. It is not clear when the changes had taken place but it already may have occurred by 1440 when demesne acreage seems to have grown dramatically.[131] Late medieval inquisitions post mortem reveal the main elements of medieval land use: there were large areas of arable with small ones of meadow and permanent pasture, and some woodland. In 1381 there were 160 a. of arable and fallow, 4.5 a. meadow, 7 a. of pasture and 32 a. of wood.[132] Most land was arable, assessments varying between 100 a. in 1349 and 160 a. arable and fallow in 1381, and then apparently growing to 408 a. in 1440,[133] the last perhaps as a result of expanding arable into the downland or shifting to a more intensive three-field system.

130 TNA, C 136/14/7.
131 TNA, C 139/96/6.
132 TNA, C 136/14/7.
133 TNA, C 135/105/7; C 136/14/7; C 139/96/6.

In the 18th century over 80 per cent of the arable land (484 a.) remained in the seven open fields (Arborough, Thatchingham, Kingsham, Painsworth, White Hill, The Down, and Musdale) which extended from the rear of the village houses or The Street to the parish boundaries everywhere but the north of the parish, where the Great Moor was situated. Musdale and Thatchingham fields abutted the main street separating the village centre houses (Glebe Cottage southward) from the northern group (that extended as far north as The Farm). A few closes lay immediately behind the houses, especially those belonging to Manor Farm that surrounded the church. Most of the closes were in the north of the parish near the Great Moor, being away from the existing open fields. Two large closes (35 a.) also belonging to Manor Farm abutted the eastern edge of the Great Moor and extended to the parish boundary. Another block of closes (35 a.) divided Arborough, Musdale, and Down fields from the southern edge of the Great Moor; they belonged to Corpus Christi College, Winchester College, and the freeholder, and in 1793 were each divided in two by the construction of the Basingstoke canal (Map 4). Arable land continued to dominate in the next century, comprising 580 a. in 1838 and 607 a. in 1872.[134]

Meadows

The presence of a small amount of meadowland (from 4.5–20 a.) is shown in the surviving inquisitions post mortem.[135] Although there were a few freehold inclosures that may have been used as meadow and small areas of meadow attached to farms after inclosure, there was no common meadowland.[136]

Woodland

An inquisition in 1349 records 32 a. of woodland that generated a small surplus, as it did in 1536.[137] By 1616, a wood known as Upgrove (43 a.), which lay in the west of the parish between Kingham and Thatchingham fields, was rented for 20s. a year.[138] In 1689–90, the wood was managed by the Corpus Christi College agent, William Hall, who repaired the gates and also sold trunks to tenants for repairs.[139] By the late 18th century the wood's value had declined and the agent, John Thorp, negotiated with a prospective tenant, Holloway, to grub up the wood and convert it to arable. The negotiation failed in 1787 because of opposition from some of the copyholders, led by Farmer Small, who claimed the right to cut 'rods and withs' there and threatened Holloway, who withdrew fearing personal injury.[140] Tenants of the manor had rights to put livestock in the wood

134 TNA, IR18/9062; OS area book, 1872.
135 TNA, C 135/105/7, C 136/14/7, C 139/96/6.
136 CCCO, MS 532/2/11–12; F/3/3/3, 22.
137 TNA, C 135/105/7; CCCO, Cb 6/2 and *passim*.
138 CCCO, Mc 13/1.
139 CCCO, Newlyn papers Hampshire, nos.11–20.
140 CCCO, Cb 16/4.

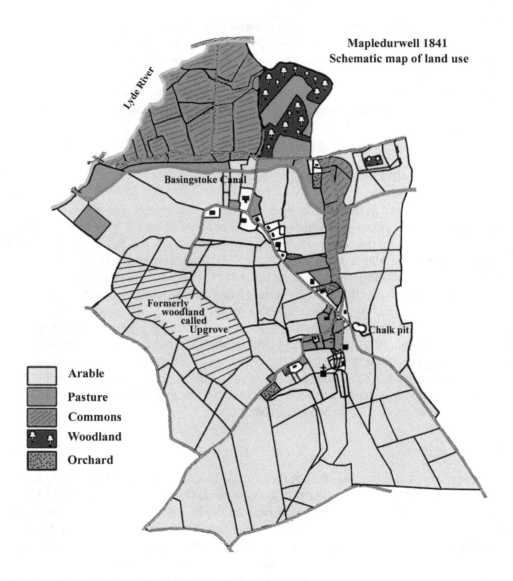

Mapledurwell 1841
Schematic map of land use

Lyde River

Basingstoke Canal

Formerly
woodland
called
Upgrove

Chalk pit

Arable
Pasture
Commons
Woodland
Orchard

Map 4   *Composite map of land use in Mapledurwell, 1841.*

at specified times. For example Hall reported in 1670 that only teggs (sheep before first shearing) were allowed in the coppice and they would be removed before 'the buds are out'.[141] In 1792 Corpus Christi College were warned that intruders were not only collecting deadwood, but also cutting down saplings of oak and other timber.[142] In 1793 Thorp successfully let the wood to James Williams to be grubbed up for arable as a new Corpus Christi College copyhold 24.[143] Thorp valued the 241 trees which were mostly

141   CCCO, F/3/3/3 p.107; CCCO, Newlyn papers, 1670, Hampshire 1–10.
142   CCCO, Cb 16/4.
143   CCCO, Cb 18/10.

small and in a bad state 'having been much cut and abused for times past' at £25 and the underwood at £23 12s. Williams, assured by the college that the tenants had no legal rights in the wood, purchased the trees and paid a fine of £162.[144] The wood was grubbed up between 1793 and 1825 but is clearly marked on the pre-inclosure map of 1797 (Map 5),[145] and in 1838 the land was still described as 'grubbed ground'.[146] There were small areas of woodland mainly on the moor in the north amounting to 20 a. in 1838 and 25 a. in 1872.[147]

Pasture, Moor, Commons

Moorland, which existed in the Middle Ages, was better documented later.[148] The north-western area of the parish comprised the Great Moor of 84 a. which by 1797 was bordered on the south by the closes north of the common arable fields, on the east by old inclosures belonging to Manor Farm, and on the north and west by the river Lyde and the turnpike road to London which became the A30.[149] The Little Moor (17 a.) lay on either side of the stream, south-east of the Great Moor, sandwiched between two open fields, Musdale and The Down. The Great Moor and the Little Moor provided communal grazing until 1863 but also had conflicting roles as a resource for peat and an area where the privileged could shoot game.[150] The copyholders and freeholders were entitled to common grazing according to the size of their holding. Their stints were specified in the inclosure award of 1797 and amounted in total to 69.[151] In addition to grazing on the moors, there were 36 a. of pasture in 1838. The moors were inclosed in 1863. In 1872 there were 138 a. of pasture in the whole parish.[152]

Peat Cutting

Some of the moor was swampy and a source of peat. Licences were granted to cut peat with restrictions designed to limit harm to grazing land. Corpus Christi College in 1752 granted a licence to Joseph Portal to dig for peat on the East Moor, which was described as 'unprofitable for herbage or tillage'. Portal was granted a seven-year licence to dig in no more than 7 a. for which he had pay £5 a year to the rent collector. All hollows were to be filled in, the site was to be fenced and ditched and any ash from burning peat was to be spread on the moor 'in a husbandlike manner for the manuring and improving the herbage of the said moor'.[153] The Basingstoke canal company was allowed in 1793 to take sods from 1.5 a. to build an embankment but only from the very swampy part of the

144 CCCO, *Acts and Proceedings*, B/4/1/2, 61.
145 CCCO, Cb 16/8.
146 CCCO, Map 120; HRO, 21M65/F7/152/1.
147 TNA, IR 18/9062; OS area book, 1872.
148 CCCO, Cb 10/3.
149 Manor Farm was CCCO, CH 15.
150 Below, Social History.
151 HRO, Q23/2/80.
152 TNA, IR 18/6092; OS Area Book, 1872.
153 HRO, 10M57/T143.

moor.[154] Unlicensed cutting of peat diminished the value of the moor and was punished in 1816 and 1820.[155] The college appointed John Wise in 1823 to supervise peat digging. However, the problem continued with reports in 1823 and 1836 that the common was much damaged by 'divers poor people cutting turf for fuel'.[156]

FARMING, 1050–1550

In 1086 Mapledurwell was part of a larger 2½-hide manor incorporating Mapledurwell itself, Up Nately, and Newnham. It then possessed six ploughlands, although seven were in cultivation suggesting some recent growth. The estate had paid £10 in 1066, which had grown to £13 in 1086. Of the ploughlands, two were in lordship, and there were twelve villagers, eight smallholders, six slaves and two mills.[157] Subsequent discussion is concerned with the smaller post-Domesday manor.

Medieval Demesne Farming

No manorial accounts survive from the period when the demesne was farmed directly by the lord and the inquisitions post mortem are lacking in detail, but some chalkland manors elsewhere in north-eastern Hampshire are better documented and provide opportunities for comparisons. The demesne was relatively small, with two ploughlands for the larger Domesday manor and 100 a. for Mapledurwell itself in 1349. The main crops were probably wheat and oats, with barley an important and expanding third crop. Tenants probably showed a greater emphasis on barley. Because of the absence of great downland pastures, sheep were probably a substantial element in farming, but there was probably no great demesne flock.[158] The village would have been closely linked to Basingstoke and its market. The town was already important within Hampshire in the early 14th century, and it grew to still greater importance with the expansion of the cloth industry in the later Middle Ages, no doubt stimulating the economy of the countryside around.

---

154 CCCO, Cb 18/10.
155 CCCO, F/3/3/8, 37, 98.
156 CCCO, F/3/3/8, 165, 404.
157 J. Munby (ed.), *Domesday Book: Hampshire*, (1982), 24–1.
158 For comparable figures see J.N. Hare, 'The Bishop and the Prior: demesne agriculture in medieval Hampshire', *Agric. Hist. Rev.*, 54 (2006), 193–6, 206; *idem*, 'Lord, tenant and the market: some tithe evidence from the Wessex Region', in B. Dodds and R. Britnell (eds), *Agriculture and rural society after the Black Death* (2008), 132–46; J.Z. Titow, 'Land and population on the bishop of Winchester's estates' (Univ. of Cambridge, PhD thesis, 1962), 134–5, 141; *idem*, 'Field crops and their cultivation in Hampshire, 1200–1350 in the light of the documentary evidence', unpublished paper in HRO, 97/M97/C1.

Medieval Tenants and Farming

Eventually the lords gave up cultivating their demesne, although the absence of documentation makes it difficult to establish when this occurred. It certainly had happened by 1488, from which date the first manorial account survives.[159] Evidence from comparable lay manors in Hampshire indicates that it probably occurred by the end of the previous century. In the later rentals, the demesne recorded as leased seems largely to have been of meadow and pasture, or of land in Newnham. Since by 1488 the customary rents had increased from £3 in 1440 to £6 3s. 1d., it seems likely that the demesne in the open fields had been divided up into new customary holdings, rather than leased as a single whole.[160] Only one of the post-medieval copyhold descriptors mentioned any demesne land, that of Arlings Farm, which was described in each court roll as 'a messuage, 8 acres and a courtland, with the demesne land thereto belonging'.[161]

FARMING, 1550–2012

Corpus Christi College, Oxford acquired the estate in 1529. Those under its lordship were a few freeholders but mainly copyholders. William Frost's rental of 1513[162] detailed six freeholds with an aggregate quit rent of 33s., exactly the same figure as that used by the assessors of *Valor Ecclesiasticus* in 1535.[163] This sum therefore represents the extent of freeholdings in the manor just before and just after the college had become lord, but only one of the quit-rents can be reconciled with precise parcels of land. There are no records of changes in the freehold tenancies after the mid 1750s, although isolated rent-book survivals from 1868–72 suggest that quit-rents totalling 15s. 10d. were still nominally payable.[164]

Most of the later Corpus Christi College manor was already held in customary tenure by copyhold when William Frost was the lord in 1513. Twelve Mapledurwell tenants occupied some 20 copyholds, fourteen of which comprised a messuage and 8 a. of land, hinting at a former regular distribution of land within the manor.[165] The remainder varied in size, suggesting amalgamation and division in earlier periods, with the largest copyhold (no. 15) belonging to Manor House (later called Manor Farm).[166] In the 17th and most of the 18th century, nine of the 17 copyholds in the parish of Mapledurwell held substantial numbers of strips in the open fields described as

---

159 CCCO, Cb 6/1.
160 TNA, C 139/96/6; CCCO, Cb 6/1.
161 CCCO, CH18. A courtland was about 30 a. in the 17th century.
162 CCCO, Cb 10/3.
163 *Valor Eccl.* II, 246.
164 CCCO, F/1/4/1–3
165 Except where specifically mentioned, the material in this section has been taken from the following sources: CCCO, Cb 10 series (rentals); CCCO, Cb 9/1 (President Randolph's Register); CCCO, Ch 11/14 ('Notes concerning Mappledurwell', *c.* 1635); CCCO, Mc 13/1 ('Description of the Estates belonging to Corpus Christi College, Oxford', *c.* 1616); CCCO, F/3/3/1–10 (court books); CCCO, F/1/1/2–12 ('Accounts of the Estates' from 1881).
166 CCCO, Cb 10/3 (William Frost's rental of 1513).

courtlands or yardlands, each amounting to about 30 a. Five held cottages and 8 a. while three comprised just cottages. Under the manor of Mapledurwell there were also two copyholds in Newnham and three in Up Nately. Two more copyholds were subsequently created in Mapledurwell, one from the common and another from the grubbed up wood in 1793.[167]

Similarly most of Winchester College land was copyhold tenure of the manor of Andwell, as shown on the map of 1806 (Map 3). Winchester College still held its lands in 1839, when their final extent, including inclosure awards, was about 48 a.[168] Two of Winchester College's copyholds were let together: one comprised a hop kiln and outbuildings with two yards or closes near the canal containing 16 a. The second included the cottage now called Addison's Farmhouse and 16 a. of land while a third included a malthouse. There was also one field in the far north-west of Mapledurwell part of a leasehold estate under the manor of Andwell.[169]

Traditionally, smaller copyholds had been exploited by the families themselves. Security of tenure during the first part of Corpus Christi College's lordship is confirmed by the fact that some families held their copyholds for many generations. In eight cases the same families, including descendants through the female line, held for more than 150 years. Exceptionally, John Nash and his descendants through the Nash and Ivold lines held copyhold No.16, centred upon the present-day Rye Cottage, for 337 years.

Sub-letting was probably unusual in the Middle Ages and the licence to have a sub-tenant in a messuage and virgate granted in 1470–1 may have resulted from its unusual location outside the village and in Eastrop.[170] As copyholds were increasingly amalgamated, sub-letting became more usual but required a licence. Twelve licences were granted between 1617 and 1622 alone.[171] In 1663 it was presented that 'No tenant had let his land without licence for longer than a year and a day nor taken in an undertenant'.[172] Sub-letting increased in the 18th and 19th centuries. The Sumner family had held their Corpus Christi College copyhold land (CH 2) for 140 years by 1799 when one John Sumner died. Thorp, the agent, reported that Sumner's death caused no change in arrangements as his widow lived in High Wycombe, Bucks and the tenant, a Mr Hutton of Basing, had long been used to going there to pay the rent. A terrier of the Corpus Christi College copyhold estate in 1808 and contemporary estate correspondence showed considerable sub-letting, especially of the 138 a. of Manor Farm belonging to Mrs Barton, widow, of which Joseph Kersley was the tenant.[173]

167 CCCO, F/3/3/6 p.427: CCCO, CH 23 was from the common, CH 24 was on the site of the grubbed up wood.
168 HRO, 21M65/F7/152/1.
169 WCM, 21 citing CC309, 21310, 23187. WCM, 1948. Conveyance under the University and Colleges Estates Act 1925, among 20th-century documents, unreferenced.
170 CCCO, A/Mc30/24. Probably the detached part of Eastrop in Up Nately.
171 CCCO, Ma 2/9.
172 CCCO, F/3/3/3, 22.
173 CCCO, Cb 16/8, 18/16.

Tenant Farming, 1500–1640

The 18 surviving wills and 17 inventories from the 16th century reveal that farming was mixed arable and pasture with sheep, the main livestock, providing wool for the local industry which continued into the 16th century. The total value of the 17 surviving inventories is £330, an average of £19. Hurdles are listed in some inventories implying managed folding on the common fields.[174] Tenant flocks were significant, but generally not large. The most valuable inventory (£60) of John Beene in 1590, listed 50 sheep.[175] The biggest flock noted in the 16th century was the 160 sheep owned by Roger Smith in 1589, a tenant of Corpus Christi and of Winchester College, but no record survives of its composition or where it was pastured.[176] There is a reference to 20 sheep being pastured in the adjoining parish of Herriard in 1547.[177] Sixteenth-century wills and inventories suggest a concentration on the breeding flock and there are very few references to wethers, probably because of the lack of large downland pastures in the parish. On the 100 a. of moorland there were stints for cows. Fodder crops of peas, vetches, oats, beans, dredge, and hay were used to supplement grazing land in the parish. Most of the copyholders possessed two cows, with one copyholder possessing ten. These numbers do not suggest purely domestic use. Pigs similarly appear, as do flitches of bacon and stores of cheese. Hens, cocks, geese and ducks were also listed together with a number of stalls of bees. There are 20 horses including five in Robert Fry's inventory of 1571 'for ploughing and carting' and one yoke of oxen.[178]

Of the 820 a. of land in the parish, approximately 526 a. were arable with 43 a. of woodland in 1616.[179] From 1600–42 15 wills and 21 inventories continue to reveal mixed farming with sheep and crops of wheat and barley, together with fodder crops. Half of the inventories include sheep with the two largest each possessing around 80; a further group had about 40 each with a few possessing about 12. Ewes and lambs are predominant, but wethers and dry sheep are recorded in two inventories and '14 teggs a wintring' in a third.[180] Numbers of cattle and pigs are small and clearly for domestic use. There are some 20 horses with no oxen, so horses were clearly used to provide the tractive power for the farm. Wheat and barley are the main crops accompanied by vetches, peas, beans, oats and hay as fodder crops. The most valuable inventory, that of Nicholas Smith in 1632 worth £322, included £150 of animals, crops and produce including cattle valued at £21, sheep at £16, horses £12, wheat and barley £48 and fodder crops £28. Smith owned lambs' wool valued at £5 16s. and was owed £150 in bonds and debts.[181] Wool was present in five inventories including one with three types of wool: fleece, lambs and locks worth in total £4 15s.[182]

---

174 For example, HRO, 1566A/52, John Taylor.
175 HRO, 1590B/04.
176 HRO, 1589AD 28, John Hulet, parson: 'Roger Smith oweth for the tithe of 8 score sheep'.
177 HRO, 1547B/050.
178 HRO, 1571B/069 (Mapledurwell probate 1518–99, Robert Frye).
179 CCCO, Langdon Map MS 532/2/11–13, Mc 13/1.
180 HRO, 1612AD 19; 1620 A/31; 1641A/10.
181 HRO, 1632A/085.
182 HRO, 1639A/207.

Tenant Farming, 1640–1740

After the Restoration, there is evident commercialisation of farming in the parish with the value of the 20 surviving inventories from 1641–1730 totalling £4734, an average of over £200. Two farmers, John Sumner who owned the freehold (d.1675, worth £732) and Roger Smith, who had succeeded the Matthew family at the manor house (d.1684, worth £713), left wealth of over £700.[183] A further six left over £200. Considerable wealth was generated by barley and malt, which was replacing wool as the main commercial product. The Smith family profited significantly from malting. In 1684 Roger Smith had 40 a. of wheat valued at £81, but his barley crop was more valuable: 44 a. valued at £89 together with 149 quarters 'of malt and barley dry and wet' valued at £141. Henry Smith (d.1691) had 150 qu. of malt valued at £150 which was just over half the value of his inventory (£291). John Sumner (d.1675) left sheep valued at £62 but his barley was worth £175 and his hops £33. A considerable number of inventories contained goods in a malthouse and querns to grind malt.[184]

Farming remained mixed arable and pasture: sheep were still important. Three farmers: Sumner, Smith and Nicholas Matthew (d.1663, £502) had sheep flocks of around 250. Matthew of Manor Farm had a total of 260 sheep valued at £69 in Mapledurwell, Up Nately and Beechinwood in Tunworth, a neighbouring parish to Mapledurwell, where his family had manorial rights and land. Manorial court presentments also reflect the large size of flocks.

By 1660, and probably for at least the previous century, farming a three-course rotation with a wheat field, barley field and a pea field was practised, the latter field being fallow where vetches, beans and oats were also sown. In 1666 owners of strips had to maintain the hedges in each field and ensure the hedges around the wheat field were complete by 14 October, those in the barley field by 1 April. The interaction between livestock and arable was very apparent in 1666 as, after the harvest, pigs were first allowed on the wheat and barley fields, followed after six days by the cattle and after a further seven to ten days the sheep were allowed to pasture. The pea field was broken up as soon as it was harvested.[185] The number of animals was strictly regulated with all animals to be marked by the owner. In 1663 every tenant had the right of commons for 40 sheep per yardland and proportionally for any other area.[186] Cow marks are listed in inventories.[187] Exceeding the stints led to a fine. Henry Smith in 1652 and John Stock in 1698 were fined for 'overcharging' the common by as many as 16 and 26 sheep respectively, suggesting relatively large tenant flocks.[188] Dung for manure was also increasingly recorded in inventories throughout the 17th century, first appearing in 1609 and being particularly, but not exclusively, a characteristic of the inventories of the wealthy farmers such as John Canner (d.1641), the freeholder, who had dung pots and dung in the gate house. In the 1660s dung carts featured for the first time. For example,

183 HRO, 1675A/09; TNA, Prob 11/378.
184 See for example, HRO, 1664 A 35, Christopher Fry.
185 CCCO, F/3/3/3, 58–62, 26 September 1666.
186 CCCO, F/3/3/3, 22.
187 For example HRO, 1620A31, William Fry.
188 CCCO, F/3/3/1, 35 and F/3/3/4, 90.

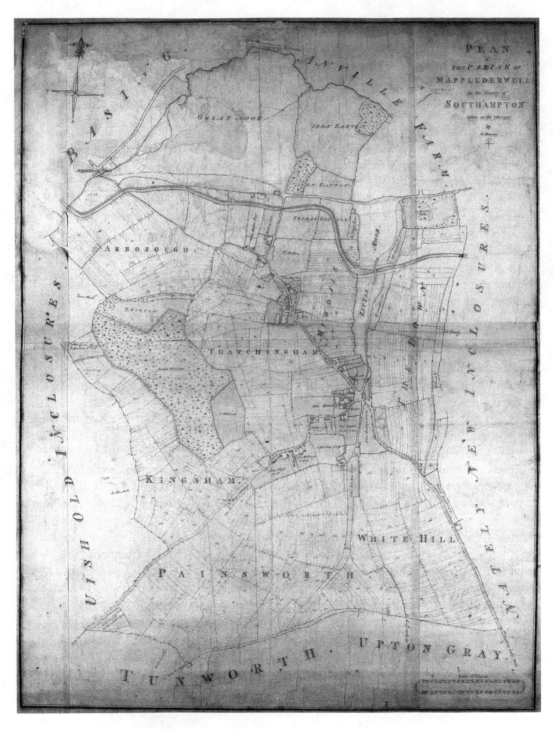

Map 5   *Pre-inclosure map of Mapledurwell, 1797.*

Nicholas Matthew of Manor Farm had two at his death in 1663, as did Roger Smith in 1684 and Henry Cooper in 1716. In total from 1600–1723 one third of the inventories recorded dung.[189] Stocks of cows and pigs remained small, suggesting their products were for local consumption only, and an entry for 'wintering the bull' in the overseers' account book for 1809 appears to indicate communal ownership of the animal.[190] Encroachments were monitored by the bailiff and by the officers of the court.[191] By the late 18th century there is considerable evidence of the poor state of the common fields, the resulting poor yields of which led to the inclosure of the common fields in 1797.

Parliamentary Inclosure of Common Fields, 1797

The inclosure of the common arable fields in 1797 was authorised by an act of parliament that also covered Basing, possibly because of the influence of the dukes of Bolton, who held substantial lands in Basing and a small messuage in Mapledurwell. The inclosure was complicated as Winchester College lamented: 'There is land in the common fields of Mapledurwell which is let with land belonging to Corpus Christi College and have been above 100 years and no one knows how to separate it.'[192] The major tenants led by John Barton of Manor Farm requested the inclosure in 1792, but it was held up for five years by the duke of Bolton.[193] The poor quality of the common fields was noted in 1794, when Thorp valued the land in the common fields at an average of 8s. per a., whereas the inclosed land was worth 12s. per a. Thorp added the 'great part of the land in the common fields is very poor, the inclosed and meadow land (25s. per a.) is pretty good, as is the coppices (12s.), but the Moore (6s.) is but of little value having been cut about very much for peat.'[194] By April 1795 a petition for inclosure was being circulated and Corpus Christi College gave its consent on 5 May 1795.[195] Despite protests about the size of fines, most tenants accepted Thorp's offer to renew their terms before inclosure.[196] The 1797 inclosure was of Basing and Mapledurwell but excluded the Great and Little Moors in Mapledurwell.[197] This award covered all seven of the Mapledurwell fields, the allotments there totalling 460 a., plus just under 7 a. of exchanges of pre-existing closes to consolidate holdings.[198] The principal landowner, Corpus Christi College, received some 85 per cent of the newly inclosed land, all of it held by copyholders apart from one small tenancy, a total of 394 a. The two copyholders from Winchester College held some 15 a. between them, and the Queen's College Oxford received just less than 9 a. for glebe, which was leased to Revd Dr Richmond, rector of Newnham and Mapledurwell. The tithes continued. There was only one freeholder with common field land, John Sumner,

189 HRO, Mapledurwell probate 1600–1723.
190 HRO, 49M67/PO2.
191 Above, Local Government.
192 WCM, 23194.
193 CCCO, Cb 18/9. The succession of a new duke led to change.
194 CCCO, Cb 18/11.
195 CCCO, Cb 18/12; Acts and Proceedings of Corpus Christi College, B/4/1/2, p.74.
196 CCCO, Cb 18/12.
197 36 Geo.III cap.16 (1795); HRO, Q23/2/80 (Mapledurwell award) and Q23/2/105 (Old Basing award).
198 Shown on 1797 pre-inclosure map of Mapledurwell, HRO, 10M57/P11.

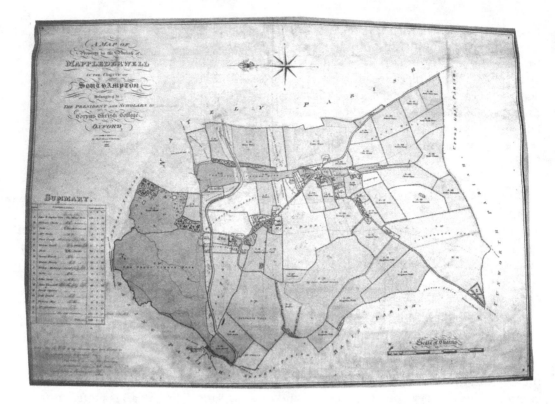

Map 6   *Post-inclosure map of Mapledurwell, 1825.*

who received just under 32 a. but who also held a copyhold from Corpus Christi College which gave him a further 37 a. Communal facilities were provided by just over half an acre for digging chalk and gravel. The open fields were divided into much smaller units in severalty but unusually all the farmhouses remained in the village streets.

From 1797–1863 there remained un-inclosed cow commons in the Great Moor (85 a.) occupying the north of the parish and the Little Moor (17 a.) towards the east of the parish with rights attached to each copyhold, freehold or leasehold.[199]

Consolidation of Farms, 1800–2000

By the mid 18th century the fixed rents and relatively low fines of copyhold appealed to the local gentry who began buying out copyhold rights in order to sub-let them at a profit. For example, John May of Huish, just beyond the western boundary, by 1752 had purchased one freehold and one copyhold property in Mapledurwell.[200] Some speculation failed. In 1829, Revd Carleton of Greywell bought out the Wise family's rights to Manor Farm for £3750, but he sold the same rights on to George Lamb nine years later for

199   HRO, Q23/2/80; CCCO, Map 120 (1825).
200   HRO, 1752 A 70; CCCO, F/3/3 series *passim*.

£1,800.[201] This system of copyholds changed after 1858, when Corpus Christi College was authorised to sell land and convert copyhold tenancies to rack-rent leases.[202] The new leases were then recorded in a series of lease books. The number of tenancies was reduced and land holdings increased in size. Some amalgamation of copyholds had occurred by 1839; for example two had been merged into one holding of 18 a. and another three into one of 50 a. held by the Small family.[203] By 1871 four farms dominated the Corpus Christi College estate: two of nearly 200 a., one of 100 a., and one of 60 a. These were Manor Farm, Thorp's Farm, Clark's Farm (The Farm),[204] and White's Farm (Garys Farm). Additionally by 1881 Joseph Addison of Mapledurwell House farmed the 60 a. of freehold land formerly attached to Webbs Farmhouse which, combined with Corpus Christi and Winchester Colleges' copyhold land, comprised a total of 104 a.[205] The copyhold land was sold off after Addison's death and by 1921 was part of the Manor Farm lease.[206] By 1939 the number of tenants had been further reduced with two main farms of over 150 a., and in 2012 there was one main farm.

The creation of larger farms from the merger of the ancient copyholds is very well illustrated by the development of the Thorp's farm in the 19th and 20th centuries. One copyhold (6) of 30 a. was extinguished and converted to a lease granted to William Thorp in 1838.[207] This was converted to a rack-rent in 1867 and let to Herbert Bradby Thorp, together with the 33 a. of another former copyhold.[208] From 1889 Thorp also acquired the 43 a. of White's Farm together with the 16 a. from two others.[209] In addition he developed an agricultural machinery business.[210] After his death in 1912 his son, Herbert Marley Thorp, continued in the ploughing business while his three daughters continued farming until their deaths in the first half of the 1960s. In 1965 Thorp's Farm was amalgamated with the manor farm, leaving only one major farm in Mapledurwell. Manor Farm had been leased from 1921 to the Hutton family who still farmed the land in 2012 and rented Garys Farm from Corpus Christi College. Manor Farmhouse was sold in 1963.[211]

The Farm (Clarke's) with 64 a., once rented in the 17th century by the Smith family and at the beginning of the 19th century by Thomas Sutton, was extinguished in 1884 and converted to rack-rent.[212] It was let first with the 50 a. of copyhold 24, the grubbed up ground, to C. Clark and then to W.E. Wright who held it until 1974 when The Farm was sold to G.E. and C.A. Saunders of Ramsdell. The sale included the farmhouse and 170 a. although the farmhouse was subsequently sold. In 1941, The Farm had 190 a. of

201 CCCO, F/3/3/8, 230 and 286; F/3/3/9, 103 relating to CCCO, CH 15.
202 Universities and Colleges Estates Act 1858, C.44.
203 CCCO, CH 9 and 20, 2, 5 and 10; also CH 21 and 22, 17 and 18; CCCO, F/3/3/8, 230 and 286; F/3/3/9, 103.
204 CCCO, CH 11.
205 Addison held CCCO CH 2 and 10 of 16 a.; TNA, RG9/709/39A; RG10/1235/77; RG11/1255/68.
206 CCCO, F/1/1/4-6; LB 57/80.
207 CCCO, LB 34/420.
208 CCCO, F/4/1; F/1/1/3; CH 19.
209 CCCO, F1/1/4 1-3; CH 4, 9 and 16.
210 Below, Crafts and Other Industries.
211 CCCO CH 4; 1924/29/29/54; 1959/65/70; 1974 (Estate Registers); LB46/107.
212 This was CCCO, CH 11.

Map 7   *Inclosure of the moors, 1863.*

which 112 a. were arable and the rest were grazing and fodder crops which were then suffering from 'infestation with rooks and wood pigeons and heavy weeds'. The freehold remained attached to Mapledurwell House, where in 1941 Col. Hamilton still farmed 30 a. of mainly barley and grassland, but he was described as a 'hobby farmer'.[213]

213 TNA, MAF 32/69.

Farming in the 19th and 20th Centuries

The 1797 inclosure of the common fields had little impact on the ratio of arable and pasture lands; however, during the 19th century there was some diversification of production, especially into watercress and later into poultry farming. The farms remained mainly arable. In 1825 Corpus Christi College held 668 a. in the parish of which 487 a. (73 per cent) were arable lands. In 1838 the soil was described as strong loam and clay with some thin parts on a chalk subsoil and that about one half of the best lands were sown with corn; a part of the thin land was kept in sainfoin and about two fifths of the remainder were sown with corn. The arable was divided into 120 a. of wheat valued at £840, and 60 a. of barley at £360. Fodder crops comprised 60 a. of oats at £297, 30 a. of beans and peas at £135, 270 a. of straw and chaff at £337, and 120 tons of hay at £420. Livestock were still dominated by sheep with 400 lambs and 700 fleeces of wool (together £345), while there were only 20 cows valued at £140.[214]

Inclosure of the Moors

The two commons or moors were inclosed in 1863 and divided into some 20 separate holdings (Map 7). The task was straightforward as the shares of each individual had already been determined in 1797. The total acreage was recorded as 98 a. consisting of the Great and Little Moors plus some small old inclosures that were incorporated in order to ensure the most efficient possible layout of the new holdings. Sixteen tenants of Corpus Christi College, two of Winchester College, and the churchwardens and overseers who had responsibility for the allotments for recreation and for the 'labouring poor' were involved in the inclosure. Both of Winchester College's lessees received additional allotments in their own right, and William White, who purchased some of Jonathan May's allotment, was himself an existing right owner, and received the second largest allotment.[215] The commissioners ordered the construction, cleansing and repair of three watercourses across the Great Moor near the streams that would serve to drain the moor as well as for water supply. The recipients of land adjoining the three watercourses were responsible for their maintenance. The costs of the process were raised by the sale of part of the land being inclosed. An allotment of 6 a. was auctioned and George Lamb of Worting paid £536 for it. Lamb also received just under 12 a. in addition to his purchase. With the completion of that inclosure, common land ceased to exist in Mapledurwell but the inhabitants were compensated with a recreation ground and allotments for the poor.[216] After the 1863 inclosure, both moors remained pasture, except for three areas on the Great Moor amounting to 7 a. that became osier beds.[217]

214 TNA, IR 18/9062.
215 HRO, 49M67/PD3.
216 Below, Social History: Prominent Families.
217 OS area book, 1872.

Watercress

Watercress growing developed widely along the streams in the north of the parish by the mid 19th century, sponsored by Mr Dudley who supplied markets in London and Liverpool.[218] An 1863 valuation of the Gary freehold included the statement that it included watercress beds, 'the value of which is only just becoming appreciated'.[219] In the same year Mr George Lamb let to Mr John Dudney of Portslade near Shoreham for 18 years, 6 a. of messuage, land and watercress bed on the East Moor, formerly part of the Little Moor which he had received in the 1863 inclosure. Dudney had to keep all property in good condition, especially the river and water courses. Watercress was to be sown in rows in husband-like fashion over all the area and hoed to keep it free from weeds.[220] In 1901 occupations included a farmer and watercress grower, two watercress labourers, and one watercress buncher. The industry continued in the 20th century. By the 1960s there were three watercress growers in the parish.[221] The watercress industry continues in 2012 on a small scale with Corpus Christi College still owning and renting one of the two remaining watercress beds.

Poultry

Poultry farming grew in importance in the 20th century, especially in 1928 when some 3,000 birds were recorded. In 1948, 880 birds were recorded with Alan Hutton described as a poultry farmer.[222]

Sheep and Arable

A dramatic decline in numbers of sheep characterised the late 19th century and early 20th century. In the 1870s there were 100 sheep, but by 1898 no sheep were recorded. Into the 20th century there were a few — about 50 from 1918 to 1938 but none by 1944, suggesting sheep farming was no longer profitable.[223] During the Second World War the priority was cereal crops rather than sheep. By 1928 and before its merger with Up Nately, Mapledurwell had slightly fewer arable acres than grazing and fodder crops. The 1941 returns for Mapledurwell seriously understate the agricultural production as the Hutton family is not included. The records for the rest of the parish show that production of wheat and barley doubled during the Second World War, but declined afterwards. Cattle rearing for milk and beef increased during the 20th century. In 2012 Manor Farm was the only major farm, part of the extensive farming operation based since 1948 in the parish of Dummer. Alan Hutton farmed 425 a. there producing wheat, barley, flax, sugar beet and turnips. He lived at Garys Farm (former Corpus Christi College copyhold 4, Fig. 11) that, with his land, was still leased from Corpus Christi College, and he owned

218 B. B. Woodward and T. Wilks, *A General History of Hampshire* (*c.* 1860), III, 284.
219 WCM, 20th-century documents, unreferenced.
220 HRO, 12M49/28.
221 TNA, RG 13/1109/36; *Kelly's Dir. Basingstoke* (1967).
222 TNA, MAF 68; *Kelly's Dir. Basingstoke* (1948).
223 TNA, MAF 68.

Figure 11 *Garys Farm, the last working farm in the village.*

Church Field and a 30 a. field on the downland). In the 1980s the Huttons reintroduced sheep to the parish. In 2012, his farm had 120 breeding ewes and 20 rams, all reared for meat. Fodder crops were still important for the sheep that were fed on root crops supplemented with hay grown in other parts of the farm holdings in Nately Scures and Dummer.[224]

THE WOOLLEN INDUSTRY, 1400–1700

The cloth industry grew in Basingstoke and its surrounding area in the 15th and early 16th centuries. By 1467, the town and its hinterland produced almost 5 per cent of Hampshire's total, and it continued to grow substantially thereafter. By 1524–5, the town had become ranked fifty-fifth in the country by taxpayers and fifty-first by wealth and was dominated by the cloth industry.[225] Mapledurwell was part of the wider industrial hinterland.

The absence of relevant medieval documentation makes it impossible to trace the early direct involvement of the villagers in cloth production but this had evidently

---

224 Information from Alan Hutton, September 2009.
225 A. Dyer, 'Ranking Lists of English Medieval Towns', in D.M.Palliser (ed.), *The Cambridge Urban History of Britain*, Vol. 1 (2000), 762, 766; J.N. Hare, 'Church-Building and Urban Prosperity on the Eve of the Reformation: Basingstoke and its Parish Church', *Hants Field Club*, 62 (2007), 185–97.

occurred by the mid 16th century, when probate inventories show the presence of people who were engaged in both agriculture and industry. Combining work in these areas was likely to have occurred earlier still. Thomas Smith (d.1552),[226] a weaver, was a tenant farmer, with 6 a. of sown crops with the spring sowing still to be done, and livestock including 30 sheep and 3 cattle, but he also had a shop with contents that included two looms and two spinning wheels, and his stores included wool and eight kersey cloths. His debt to a Londoner for wool suggests that he received the wool and was paid on completion of the cloth.[227] John Taylor,[228] a fuller who died in 1566, showed a similar interaction of agriculture and cloth trades. He came from a family that was prominent in the village from the 1480s. In 1487–8 one Taylor had amassed a messuage and virgate, two gardens a cottage and 3 a., and another held a messuage and 8 a.[229] John Taylor remained an agricultural producer with 16 a. of sown land and his own livestock and agricultural equipment including eight hurdles presumably for holding his sheep, but he diversified into industry with a shop and the equipment needed for fulling and finishing the cloth, including three pairs of shears, a shear board and press and eight burling irons.[230] An active cloth industry is also suggested by the presence of spinning wheels for wool and linen in eight of the inventories.[231]

Later inventories suggest some diversification from cloth production into linen and ropemaking, probably as the cloth industry ran into difficulties. Robert Fry, a husbandman, possessed ten pounds of hemp in 1571. The inventory of John Smith (d. 1596) does not specify his occupation but he had a horse, a pack saddle and riding saddle, a spinning wheel, one stone of hemp, eight pounds of linen and '13 pieces of women's wearing linen clothes'. Smith also had ropes 'sold and to be sold' valued at £1.[232] In the 17th century the difficulties of the industry are probably reflected in the declining numbers of spinning wheels within the village, only three inventories recording them: one specifically for wool and two for linen.[233]

CRAFTS AND OTHER INDUSTRIES

In the 16th and early 17th centuries, apart from clothworkers, the usual range of rural craftsmen were present including carpenters and a shoemaker. John Wylde in 1580 possessed a wide range of carpentry tools including axes, squares, chisels, augurs, and planes, together with timber, wood, and gate hinges. His inventory included debts for a number of days' work.[234] From 1600 there were also inventories of a wheelwright, blacksmith, tailor, and two sievemakers. The blacksmith and the tailor had inventories valued at £35 and £37, the wheelwright and sievemaker at £29, and the carpenter at £16.

226   Variants of this name are Smyth and Smythe.
227   HRO, 1552 U/59/1.
228   Variants of this name are Tailor, Tayler and Taylour.
229   CCCO, Cb 10/1.
230   HRO, 1566A/52.
231   HRO, 1543B/065; 1552U/59; 1555 U/69/1; 1566A/52; 1580A/96.
232   HRO, 1596AD 62.
233   HRO, Mapledurwell probate 1609 A72/1,1664/A/03.
234   HRO, 1580A/96.

The carpenter and the blacksmith had numerous tools of their trades. All the craftsmen combined their trade with some farming.

Milling

Although there does not seem to have been a mill within the manor itself, millers were presented before the manorial courts for excessive charges. In 1512 John Jak who leased a watermill at Andwell, just outside Mapledurwell's north-west boundary, from Winchester College was presented: it may be that although physically outside the manor, it was nevertheless regarded as part of it.[235] A court presentment in May 1663 recorded that there 'is no Custom Mill where the tenants are bound to grind their corn'.[236] Tenants may have ground corn at Andwell. Richard Ifould of Mapledurwell, who died in 1614, was a millwright, and it is possible that he serviced Andwell mill.[237] In 1707 a rope-maker, James Canner, left monetary bequests in his will which totalled £130: he left to his son, John, 'all my working tooles: and cartes.... two pair of best scales, all my weights, two pair of my best cale coomes with Furnace, Table, Frame and pair of Andirons standing in my kitchen Together with my Chest, Bushell measure and all my boardes in the warehouse chamber now in his possession in the Angel Inn, Basingstoke... with the barrel which is in the buttery of my dwelling house'.[238]

In the later 18th century the economy remained mainly agricultural, supported by innkeepers, blacksmiths, and a carpenter. One surprising occupation is that of collarmaker. John Drew (d. 1763) left to his son, John, 'a messuage or tenement garden, orchard, shop, land and premises; all his tools including his horse and cart and the pump furnace'. Drew also left £150 for part of his wife's annual annuity of £10: the rest to be paid by his son. He also left bequests of £130 to his children, but unfortunately his will gave no indication of the extent of his trading area.[239]

Smiths

The blacksmith trade remained in one family for a considerable period. In 1670, it was presented to Corpus Christi College manorial court that Nicholas Gary had built a shop upon the common, and in 1692 the shop was confirmed as a smithy.[240] Luke and John Gary were described as blacksmiths in their wills of 1780 and 1815,[241] but, by 1833, members of the family were described as yeomen. William Gary's will of that year mentions his 'freehold Messuage of Tenement and Blacksmiths Shop ... now in the occupation of John Gidge'.[242] The Gary freehold is now known as The Willows. Smithies operated by William Benham and George Gidge existed on both the Great and Little

---

235 CCCO, Cb 1/4.
236 CCCO, F/3/3/3, 22.
237 HRO, 1614A/065.
238 HRO, Mapledurwell probate 1500–1707.
239 HRO, 1763A/37.
240 CCCO, F/3/3/3, 107; F/3/3/4, 59.
241 HRO, 1780A/038; HRO 1815 A28.
242 HRO, 1833 A23.

Commons in 1841 and 1851, but it appears that only George Gidge, at the Gary freehold, was practising the trade in 1861, 1871, and possibly 1881.[243] Subsequently, the presence of blacksmiths was intermittent. No blacksmith is mentioned in either of the 1891 and 1901 censuses, but a further smithy had been established between 1871 and 1911, and possibly replaced the facility operated by the Gidges.[244] It stood on Winchester College land on the extreme north-eastern boundary of the parish and was part of the tenancy of its Priory Farm estate in neighbouring Andwell.[245] It was said to be derelict in September 1948.[246] The Brown family appear listed as blacksmiths in various directories between 1920 and 1932.[247]

Malting

Malting had become commercial after 1660 and continued to be important in the 19th century. Robert Small, a tenant of Winchester College and Corpus Christi sub-let his malthouse near the ford to Thomas Hutton, maltster in 1805.[248] William Clark, maltster, operated this malthouse for more than 20 years in the mid 19th century.[249] A small part of Kingham Field adjoining Upgrove had been inclosed by 1797 and was known as Hop Garden Close; this, together with a hop kiln located on Winchester College land, suggests the presence of a small brewing industry in the village.[250] In the first half of the 19th century trades included the blacksmith, two innkeepers of Mapledurwell Hatch, together with a shoemaker, a cordwainer, a servant, a brickmaker, and a sawyer.[251] In 1872 were also three osier beds amounting to 7 a., together with streams and three ponds. The osier beds may account for the basket maker who was lodging at the Kings Head in 1871.[252]

Farm Machinery

By the early 20th century, Thorp's business hiring out steam powered farm machinery and drivers disturbed the rural tranquility of Mapledurwell. Herbert B. Thorp, established as a farmer and watercress grower by 1878, expanded his business by 1889 to become a threshing machine proprietor. This was a substantial business with a turnover of £500–900 a year from 1890–1903 for threshing wheat, barley, oats, beans, peas and dredge in the local area.[253] Thorp continued in this activity until 1907 when he was joined by his son, Herbert M. Thorp. The steam ploughs and operating teams frequently

243 TNA, HO 107/385/12/4 and 7; HO 107/1681/37-38; RG 9/709/38; RG 10/1235/75; RG 11/1255/66.
244 OS Map 1:10560, sheet XIX (1911 edn); R. W. F. Potter, *Hampshire Harvest* (1984), facing page, 1; OS Map 1:10560, sheet XIX (1871 edn).
245 WCM, 21310.
246 Valuation and report by Pink & Arnold, of 3 September 1948 in an unreferenced bundle in the Winchester College archive. The site is at SU 691521, but the building no longer exists.
247 *Kelly's Dir. Hants* (1920–32).
248 Winchester College, CH 5.
249 TNA, HO 107/1681/39;TNA, Prob 11/1447; RG 9/709/38; RG 10/1235/75.
250 HRO, 10M57/P11; WCM, 21310, 39.
251 HRO, 49M67/PR7.
252 OS Area book, 1872, TNA: PRO, RG10/1235/77.
253 *White's Dir. Hants* (1878); HRO, 66A11/1.

worked away during the week in north Hampshire villages.[254] The son traded at least until 1931, by which time his enterprise included steam ploughing, threshing, hauling and baling, as well as dealing in brick, sand, and gravel.[255]

The use of machinery and motor vehicles was highlighted in 1927 when Joseph Houtet was described as a motor engineer, and in 1931 when Alan Hutton, a former poultry farmer, had become a haulage contractor. The possible importance of that new business is revealed in the much more diverse occupations of the fathers of children admitted to the village school in the 1920s: of the 51 admissions, nine fathers were engine drivers, one was a lorry driver, three were engineers and one was a boiler maker.[256]

COMMERCE AND SERVICES

In the 19th century, shopkeeping activities were carried out from existing cottages. For example, John Hutchins was keeping shop in a cottage now identified as Maple Cottage at least from 1839 to 1850, and John Moore was a shopkeeper in 1808, though the type of shop was not specified.[257] From 1859 to 1861, William Clark was also running a grocery business from his malthouse.[258] Henry Ackland was described as a baker and grocer in 1861 and 1871. James Moody was listed as a baker/shopkeeper in 1841 and 1851, with premises just off The Street, which appears now to be the old Post Office[259] at the northern end of the village.[260] A post office opened by 1897, but offered limited financial services.[261] The post office (Fig. 12) was the only village shop in the 20th century, and Joseph Ackland combined the occupations of sub-postmaster and baker in 1901.[262] Ackland continued in his post at least until 1915, but was replaced by Catherine Paice by 1920, when the premises had become a 'Post and Telegraph Office'.[263] In 1939 Mrs Paice was listed as shopkeeper and postmaster and by 1958 as shopkeeper and confectioner. The post office finally closed in 1975.[264] The building was derelict by 1998, but its restoration was completed in 2008.[265] Since 1975 there have been no shops in the parish.

254 R. W. F. Potter, *Hampshire Harvest* (1984), 18–19.

255 *Kelly's Dir. Hants* (1907 and later editions, *passim*).

256 *Kelly's Dir. Hants* (1927 and 1928); HRO 115M87/A1.

257 HRO, 21M65 F7/152/1–2; 50M63/B1/2; 1808AD/49.

258 *White's Dir. Hants & IOW* (1859); TNA:PRO, RG9/709/38

259 CCCO, CH 20.

260 TNA, HO 107/385/12/7; HO 107/1681/42; HRO, 10M57/SP459.

261 OS Map, 1: 2500 Sheet XIX, (1912 edn); *Kelly's Dir. Hants* (1898 and later editions, *passim*).

262 TNA, RG 13/1109/35–36.

263 *Kelly's Dir. Wiltshire, Dorset and Hampshire* (1920 and later editions, *passim*).

264 *The Villager* (1975) [parish magazine].

265 S. Waight, personal comment and photographs.

Figure 12 *The Old Post Office in 1915.*

Public Houses

The Hatch

Situated at Mapledurwell Hatch, it is the older and larger of the two public houses in the parish. Originally known as the King's Head, it is situated on former Corpus Christi College copyhold (23) that was created out of the moor around 1729.[266] The cottage originally built on the site was later absorbed into or replaced by a large house, but it is not known when the house was built or first used as a public house or inn. However, John Hall became the copyholder in 1736,[267] and he was described as inn holder of Mapledurwell and Hatch in 1766.[268] It was known as the King's Head at least by 1788, when the copyhold rights were to be sold by auction and it was described thus:

> a substantial, well brick-built Messuage, with a Garden, inclosed by a quick fence, stocked with fruit trees, and through which runs a pleasant trout stream; coach house, and good stabling for twenty horses; also two pieces or parcels of excellent water meadow ground, containing six acres, or thereabouts, adjoining to the garden.[269]

266 CCCO, F/3/3/4, 214.
267 CCCO, F/3/3/5, 38.
268 HRO, 1766A/045.
269 *Hampshire Chronicle*, XV, no.806, 3.

Figure 13 *The Hatch public house, a cottage enclosed from the moor used by travellers by road and canal.*

From 1794 onwards, the site was ideally situated for its purpose. Not only was it on the main turnpike road to London out of Basingstoke, but, from the opening of the Basingstoke canal in that year, it was conveniently situated in a loop of the canal to serve the bargemen and others using it. The copyhold was extinguished by 1868 and The Hatch was leased to Thomas and John May of Basingstoke, brewers, until 1959 when Simmonds Brewery bought out the Mays. Courage bought out Simmonds and finally purchased The Hatch from Corpus Christi in 1967.[270]

The Queen's Head

Now known as The Gamekeepers (Fig. 15), it was mentioned in 1859 and again in the 1861 census when the occupier Joseph Phillips was described as an innkeeper and shoemaker. Phillips, with his wife Elizabeth, had occupied the same site in 1841 and 1851 as a shoemaker, and bricks around the fireplace inscribed 'JP 1854' and 'EP 1854' imply that it was a significant year.[271] No boarders were recorded in the census of 1861 or 1871, but there were several in 1881, 1891 and 1901.[272] The public house retained the name Queen's Head at least until 1931.[273]

---

270 CCCO, LB 49/27.
271 G. Russell-Cave, personal comment.
272 TNA, RG 9/709/39A; RG 10/1235/77; RG 11/1255/68; RG 12/958/90; RG 13/1109/36.
273 *Kelly's Dir. Hants* (1899 and later edns, *passim*).

Commercial Development since 2000

In the early 21st century commerce has developed mainly on the northern edge of the moor along the main road to the east of The Hatch public house, where a small industrial estate has been constructed; some of its 11 units were proving hard to let in 2012. To the east of the industrial estate is the large Conkers garden centre with a café designed to attract passing trade. Other developments in 2012 included offices, one offering technology solutions. There were also boarding kennels, together with some small-scale businesses operated from homes.

FROM THE MIDDLE AGES Mapledurwell was a farming community with a number of related trades. In the absence of a resident lord, parish affairs were managed by the leading freeholders and copyholders that appeared at the manorial court, served as churchwardens and overseers of the poor, and witnessed wills. The location of all settlement along or near The Street probably fostered a sense of community. By the early 20th century many of the villagers were poor and their housing far from ideal. But from the 1960s the nature of the residents changed. Professionals, attracted by the expansion of Basingstoke and the ease of commuting to London, modernised, preserved, and improved many of the older houses. The school closed in 1939, but several public buildings including the church, the village hall, and two inns continued to provide a focus for village life.

SOCIAL STRUCTURE

The medieval landlords were probably non-resident, and non-residence was certainly the case from 1529 when Corpus Christi College Oxford became lord of the manor. Representatives from the college made progresses in Hampshire during which they held manorial courts in Mapledurwell to admit tenants. The college employed a steward to administer their estate affairs, but the day-to-day business of the parish was largely managed by the wealthiest tenants, and by the one significant freeholder who from about 1802 inhabited a gentry residence at the northern end of the village street.[274]

The Village Community, 1350–1550

The period showed two conflicting trends. The Black Death of 1348–9 devastated the population, whose numbers remained low until the 16th century. By contrast the growth of the Basingstoke cloth industry in the 15th and early 16th centuries increased demand both for agricultural products and for people to work in the industry. A group of substantial families emerged who accumulated land and were active in agriculture, industry, and the running of the village.

    One of the effects of plague was to shift the balance of the land market between the lord and his tenants, and to open up new opportunities for the accumulation of tenancies. Rentals in 1487–8 and 1513 and the records for the subsidy levied in 1524–5 reveal something of that society. By 1513 there had emerged a group of people, such

274 TNA, PROB 11/1572; WCM, 21309.

as William Kinge, Thomas Kinge,[275] Richard Taylor, and John Canner (also a major freeholder) who held several customary holdings and were important figures in the running of village and court.[276] Some cottages may have been sub-let, but the licence granted in 1470–1 to have a sub-tenant in a messuage and virgate in Eastrop may have been exceptional and due to its location outside the village.[277] There was also considerable fluidity of population, although the appearance of this may have been accentuated by the practice of sub-letting; almost half the surnames found in the 1487 rental were not recorded in 1513.[278]

Mapledurwell had eight taxpayers in 1327, which, with its low tax assessment in 1334, suggests it was one of the poorest and smallest of the settlements in the hundred of outer Basingstoke.[279] By the 1525 taxation, however, it had become the third wealthiest and fourth most populous settlement in the hundred.[280] The number of households in the village had risen to 35 by 1524–5, although there were only 22 tenants, suggesting an active world of sub-letting, at least of spare cottages and on the freehold tenancies. The high level of some of the assessments from £10 to £30 may suggest the presence of non-agricultural earnings. William Kinge, assessed at £30, was a substantial tenant holding the equivalent of two virgates as well as being Frost's bailiff; Kinge's holding became the chief tenancy, the Manor Farm.[281] Below Kinge came William Fry with a messuage and 16 a. in 1513[282] and an assessment for John Fry of £20, Thomas Tanner with £19 10s., and fourth John Tanner with £10.[283] Half the villagers were assessed at £4 or above, the lowest assessment being for seven at £1.[284]

Prominent Families

Some village families became prosperous and influential. The Canners were the leading tenant family of the village for almost 200 years from 1450–1641. Initially they seem little different from other villagers. William Canner was engaged in a fight with another man in 1425, and a John Canner overstocked with pigs in 1436. It was probably the same William Canner who brewed and broke the assize of ale and was fined for non-attendance in 1450, when a Nicholas Canner acted as ale-taster.[285] The family became active in the neighbouring town of Basingstoke, with Roger Canner acting as under-bailiff in 1464 and in 1481 only six men of the town had higher assessments of their goods. John Canner was among the tenants who helped within the town and lordship

---

275 Variants from the 15th–20th centuries are Kynge and King.
276 CCCO, Cb 10/3.
277 CCCO, Mc 30/24.
278 CCCO, Cb 10/1; 10/3.
279 TNA, E 179/173/4 (HRO microfilm 362a).
280 R. Glasscock (ed.), *The Lay Subsidy of 1334* (British Academy, Records of Economic and Social History), 2nd ser., ii (1975); J. Sheail (ed R. Hoyle), *The Regional Distribution of Wealth in England*, List and Index Society, ii (1998), 119.
281 CCCO, Cb 10/3.
282 CCCO, Cb 10/3.
283 Spelt Tanner in the subsidy.
284 CCCO, Cb 10/3; TNA, E179/183.
285 Baigent and Millard, *Basingstoke*, 265; CCCO Cb1/2.

and subsequently acted as one of the town's eight representatives in a dispute with John Wallop, a neighbouring lord.[286] As well as serving as one of the two bailiffs, the principal town officers in 1490–1, Thomas Canner had sold tallow and wax candles in 1464. In the Mapledurwell courts of 1512 and 1516 both John Canner and Thomas Canner were among the influential men who made up the 12 jurors.[287] The family were also active elsewhere in the area, John Canner holding a fulling mill in Andwell in 1399.[288] They were leading tenants in Mapledurwell, as in 1487–8, 1513,[289] and in 1525.[290]

Two other families formed part of the long-standing village elite, the Kinges and the Taylors. The Kinges were already present in 1450 when Thomas was involved in a complaint about his pigs. In 1486–7, John Kinge was reeve and a large-scale tenant with a virgate, another 8a. and an additional close and meadow. William Kinge had accumulated even more in 1513, was an influential figure in the 1512 court, and was bailiff in 1528. While he was the highest assessed man in the village in 1525, three other members of the family were also highly assessed at £4 each.[291] Walter Taylor in 1454 was already one of the village leaders in a dispute with the rector, and held a tenement and 8 a. with an additional garden in 1487–8. In the same year Richard Taylor had amassed a messuage and virgate, two gardens, a cottage and 3 a.[292] Richard retained his properties in 1513 and was among the important players in the lives of the village, acting as juror and assessor to the courts in 1516, before his death in 1518.[293] It was his successor, another Richard, who had the sixth highest assessment in 1525.[294] Richard's successor John (d. 1566) remained an agricultural producer but diversified into industry with a shop and the equipment needed for fulling and finishing the cloth.[295]

The Smiths were more recently arrived, not present in 1487–8 but at Mapledurwell in 1512 and 1513 when a member of the family was both a juror and a tenant of a messuage and 8 a. Three members of the family were in the top half of the assessments in 1525.[296] A later Smith was a weaver and farmer, and possessed the largest and most highly valued flocks. The family later rose to even greater importance within the village.

Mapledurwell in the 17th and 18th Centuries

There were no resident gentry, although the marquis of Winchester owed suit to the manorial court for a small property that he rented out. Local gentry took an interest in the parish at least from 1751 when John May, gentleman, from Huish, then in a detached

286 *ibid*, 287, 293–4, 436, 29, 302, 309.
287 CCCO, Cb1/4 & 5.
288 WCM, 3092.
289 CCCO, Cb 10/1; 10/3.
290 TNA, E 179 173/183.
291 CCCO, Cb 1/2, 10/1, 10/3, 1/4, 6/2; TNA PRO E179/173/183.
292 CCCO, Cb 10/1, 1/4, 10/3; TNA, E179/173/183.
293 CCCO, Cb 10/3; 1/5; HRO, 1518B/39.
294 TNA, E 179/173/183.
295 Above, Economic History, Crafts and Other Industries.
296 CCCO, Cb 10/1; HRO 1566A/52.

part of Nately Scures parish, on the western boundary of Mapledurwell, purchased copyhold property in Mapledurwell.[297]

The gap between the better off and poorer tenants is revealed in surviving tax returns, estate records, and inventories. The hearth tax assessment of 1665 recorded 21 chargeable properties with a total of 42 hearths and 15 non-chargeable properties, each with one hearth. The major freeholder was John Sumner, assessed with four hearths: he had purchased the land previously owned by generations of the Canner family. Corpus Christi College copyholders, Widow Matthew and Henry Smith, were apparently even more prosperous with five hearths each. Joan Matthew, widow of Gregory, was the tenant of the Manor Farm, chief Corpus Christi College copyhold, comprising some 150 a. of closes, open field and pasture land.[298] Gregory Matthew and the Hall family, who became tenants of Manor Farm at the end of the 17th and into the 18th century, were substantial farmers with interests outside Mapledurwell in Newnham and Tunworth parishes. Matthew and later Hall, held the two Corpus Christi College copyholds of Hooklands in Newnham at a rent of £3 per annum.[299] In Tunworth Matthew held pasture called Beechinwood, where he kept some of his sheep flock, and Joane Hall, widow, held the manor of Tunworth, her son William being described as a gentleman.[300]

The Smith family also rose in importance. When Henry Smith's father died in 1645 his house comprised a hall, two chambers, a buttery with loft over, kitchen, and a malthouse.[301] The Smiths sponsored the only private charity in 1678.[302] Roger Smith, recorded with three hearths, was also wealthy, holding the second largest copyhold, The Farm, from Corpus Christi College, and a copyhold from Winchester College. At his death in 1684 his goods were valued at £713 derived from farming and malting.[303] Smith's business contacts were in Basingstoke and Reading, a much wider area than other Mapledurwell testators of that period. He was a Quaker and asked to be buried at the Quaker burial place in Alton.[304] Six parishioners were assessed at two hearths including Christopher Fry, who is in the middle range of property holdings from Corpus Christi College paying 11s. 6d rent for a messuage, 8½ a., a toft or cottage called Mills and 3 a., a close called Millwards, and one courtland. The non-chargeable 15 hearths at the lower end of the social scale were cottagers renting for 1s. to 2s., and sub-tenants without legal tenancy.[305]

A Divided Society, 1800–2000

The social divisions in Mapledurwell remained evident in 1811 when the population of 172 comprised 40 families living in 35 houses; of those, 9 were described as principally

297 HRO, 1752A/70. John May purchased Corpus Christi College copyhold 20; CCCO F/3/3/5, 141.
298 *Hearth Tax*, 236; CCC F/3/3/3, 45; HRO, Q23/2/80.
299 CCCO, Cb 9/1; F/3/3/3, 45.
300 HRO, 44M69/D1/9/8 (1–10).
301 HRO, 1645A 47/2. CCCO, CH10.
302 *Parl. Papers*, 1826 (382), 14, 400–2; below, Charities and Welfare.
303 TNA, PROB 4/8604; CCCO, CH11.
304 Below, Religious History.
305 *Hearth Tax*, 236.

involved in agriculture, 4 in trade, manufactures and handicrafts, and there were 27 labouring families, presumably agricultural labourers.[306] The nine families involved in agriculture included the two principal Corpus Christi College copyholders of the Manor Farm and The Farm, and the freeholder, now Thomas Page. All were assessed at over £8 for land tax.

The copyhold tenants varied from the rich to the relatively poor. The copyholder of the Manor Farm was John Barton but it was sub-tenanted to Joseph Kersley. Thomas Sutton tenanted and lived at The Farm where he employed a housekeeper and a servant.[307] He also held the two Winchester College copyholds near his farmhouse,[308] and in 1817 he left £750 together with annual annuities amounting to £45. The May family from Huish also acquired two copyhold properties in Mapledurwell.[309] The larger one was a 6 a. field on the western boundary of the parish adjoining their farm at Huish. The tithes, property of the Revd John Richmond, valued at £9, were sub-let with the glebeland to Robert Small, who also had a small freehold from Winchester College and a Corpus Christi College copyhold (6) of farmhouse and 40 a. Of the craftsmen, the Gary family of blacksmiths with freehold and copyhold land in Mapledurwell and Up Nately, some of which was sublet, were also influential and prosperous. When John Gary died in 1815, shortly after his father, he left £50 to his servant, John Gidge and 4s. per week for life to his housekeeper.[310] Nine copyholds were assessed at less than £2.

One copyholder of the nine might have offended others in the parish: Mary Meddings in 1836 provided for her four legitimate children and also for her four illegitimate children who were surnamed Costin. As a tenant of some 30 a. from Corpus Christi College with a probate value of no more than £450, perhaps she did not remarry in order to prevent her rights in the copyhold and those of her first husband's children being transferred to a new husband.[311] This is perhaps a reminder of economic considerations overcoming the demands of social respectability.

In 1851, 50 per cent of the workforce were agricultural labourers. The proportion had only declined slightly ten years later. The older style of service in husbandry, where servants lived in the farmhouse, also survived. For example, Manor Farm in 1851 had four agricultural carters and one shepherd living in as servants but by 1861 only the sub-tenant, Matthew Ridge and his family, lived in the farmhouse. The Farm, occupied by the Clark family, had three agricultural carters and one agricultural labourer living in and ten years later two carters, a shepherd and a labourer, but in general the scarcity in the record of domestic servants reflected the modest status of much of the farming community. Only the occupier of Mapledurwell House, the maltster, and two of the farmers had one domestic servant each in 1851.[312] This decline in domestic service may also have been reflected in the construction of the new cottages in the late 19th century in Kembers Lane and Frog Lane.

306 HRO, 49M67/P02.
307 HRO, 1817B/69.
308 WCM CH 1 and 2.
309 HRO, 1752 A 70.
310 TNA, PROB 11/1576; HRO 1822A/26.
311 HRO, 1836 B/62 and HRO/12M49.
312 TNA, HO 107/1681.

An entrepreneurial farming family, the Thorps, played a leading role in village society in the late 19th century and first half of the 20th century. H. B. Thorp and his son, H. M. Thorp of Garys Farm, Tunworth Road, both farmed and operated a steam traction business.[313] They were deeply involved in parish and school business. For 50 years after H. B. Thorp's death in 1912 his three unmarried daughters cared for the church, the sick, played the organ, served as churchwardens, taught in the Sunday school, and helped with the village school. The youngest, Miss Nora Thorp, also researched the history of the village.[314]

THE LIFE OF THE COMMUNITY

Social divisions in the parish were reflected in leisure activities. Shooting game on the Great Moor was always the preserve of the better off and frequently alienated the farming community. The rights to shoot game (deputation) belonged to the lord of the manor but as Corpus Christi College was a non-resident lord they were offered to local gentry, who enjoyed them with their friends and also sent game to the table of the college president. Joseph Addison (d.1888) of Mapledurwell House, for example, possessed guns and a game bag.[315] In addition to shooting, two fox hunts, Sir John Cope's and the Vyne, were within easy distance. There were also two packs of harriers in the immediate vicinity.[316]

A dispute broke out early in the college's lordship when servants of Thomas Haydock, who had the rights to shoot for game, especially partridge, on Mapledurwell manor, were attacked by nine men from (Old) Basing, who claimed in their defence that they were protecting the rights of the lords of the manor.[317] In the late 17th century the bailiff William Hall complained to the president that 'My Lord Marquis [of Winchester] comes almost dayly a hunting hither and last week brake one of the coppice gates all to pieces so that I was forced to make a new one'.[318] The popularity of the deputation of the manor with the local gentry was evident in the numbers of applications to the college, including one from Lord Spencer Chichester, following the death of the holder Charles May in 1808. The award to Joseph Russell of Hoddington House in nearby Upton Grey was unpopular with Mapledurwell farmers who petitioned the college in 1809 and 1810 about damage done to their crops by Russell and his friends and servants while hunting.[319] The college asked Russell to let the leading tenants hunt as they traditionally had done. Russell apparently complied.[320] He meanwhile kept the college gentlemen happy by sending pheasant and partridge to Oxford and rebuilding stocks on the moor, which he stated had been overused before.

---

313 Above, Economic History, Crafts and Other Industries.
314 R. W. F. Potter, *Hampshire Harvest*, (1984), 36–7.
315 HRO, 50M/63/B1/32
316 HRO, 10M57 C113.
317 TNA, STAC 2/25/308. 22.04.1509-28.01.1547.
318 CCCO, Newlyn Correspondence (Unreferenced), 19 October 1687.
319 CCCO, CB 16/9; 18/23, 24, 25.
320 CCCO, Cb 16/9, 8 September 1808. The copyholder of the Manor Farm was the non-resident Widow Barton.

Community Activities and Buildings

The people of Mapledurwell, at least until 1940, enjoyed their rural location, with the fun of harvesting and fruit picking which fostered community spirit. Its appeal in the first half of the 20th century was captured by Robert Potter, later an author and lecturer at the University of Liverpool, who frequently stayed with Bill Prince, his grandfather, in Jasmine Cottage.[321] In the late 19th and early 20th centuries the children enjoyed a five-week harvest holiday in the summer, sometimes divided into two distinct periods, one in August and one in late September for potato lifting, as well as a two week break at Christmas and the traditional religious feast-days; a May Queen, chosen from the schoolgirls, presided over the May Day celebrations. In addition there were Sunday school outings, which went farther afield as the availability of motorised transport improved; for instance, in July 1922 the children were taken to Lee-on-the-Solent near Portsmouth.[322]

More structured facilities for sports and outdoor pursuits were provided for all parishioners in 1863 when the commons were inclosed. A two-acre plot was allotted in trust to the churchwardens and overseers of the poor of the parish on the southern edge of the Great Moor adjoining the old road from Mapledurwell Hatch to Greywell in the west of the parish as a place for 'exercise and recreation' for the inhabitants. The parish council inherited the recreation ground, and cricket was being played there in 1885 when a charge was made for rolling the pitch.[323] The cricket pitch was still in use in the 1930s.[324] When the M3 motorway was driven through the recreation ground in 1971, a replacement was constructed to its south on the south end of the moor, but in 2012 cricket was no longer played and the football pitch was rented to a team from outside the parish.

From the late 19th century the village schoolroom was used for indoor social activities including a temperance tea, mothers' union meeting, jumble sales, various performances, and entertainments for the children.[325] By 1923 many events had moved to the village hall or 'parish room' opposite Addison's Cottage on the main street which was formally rented from Corpus Christi College for 10s. per annum from at least 1925, with H. M. Thorp and Mrs I. L. M. Bryant acting as trustees. The parish room was built of corrugated iron and had no electricity. The land around it was in need of fencing in 1945.[326] The room was inadequately heated by an oil stove and lit by oil lamps. Mapledurwell and Up Nately had a Women's Institute (WI) with about 20 members who met in the hall from 1952 to 1968, and enjoyed many craft activities, as well as being entertained by garden parties at Mapledurwell House. By 1968 attendance had fallen to 16, so the Institute was suspended with some sadness as 'as there is nothing else in the two scattered villages'.[327] In 1967 the WI were said to be the only users of the hall,

---

321 Potter, *Hampshire Harvest*, 1–40.
322 HRO, 115M87/LB3, 3.
323 HRO, 49M67/PV1, 1–2 (the earliest surviving accounts start in 1885).
324 OS Map 1:2500 sheet XIX (1932 and 1939 edns).
325 HRO, 115M87/LB 1 and 2.
326 OS Map 1:2500 sheet XIX (1939 edn); HRO, 115M87/LB 3 pp. 12, 41; HRO, 42M91 PX27/1 and 2.
327 HRO, 96M96/63.

Figure 14 *The village hall, 2012.*

Figure 15 *The Gamekeepers, a mid 19th-century inn.*

which was demolished shortly afterwards and replaced by a house. A new village hall for Mapledurwell and Up Nately opened in June 1975 (Fig. 14), followed by a sports pavilion behind the village hall in 1980.[328] In 2012 social life was focused on the village hall, sports pavilion with tennis courts, and the two local pubs, The Gamekeepers (Fig. 15) and The Hatch (Fig. 13).

EDUCATION

Mapledurwell had a day school from 1828 to 1939, which was briefly reopened from 1940–3 as a wartime emergency measure when evacuees were sent to the village. In 2012 apart from nursery schooling, pupils are educated outside the parish.

Educational Provision before 1860

No day or Sunday school existed in 1819, when it was reported that 'the poor have not sufficient means of education, but are desirous of possessing them.'[329] A day school was in operation from 1828, and there were 14 children on the roll in 1835 with instruction paid for by parents.[330] In 1851 twelve children of eight years and over were scholars. Jane Monger, the 45-year-old wife of an agricultural labourer, was the schoolmistress.[331] In 1859 Ann Jewell was schoolmistress, while Matilda Scuffel, the 55-year-old wife of a garden labourer, held the post in 1861 when 25 of the village children were described as scholars.[332]

The Village School, 1860–1938

Mapledurwell school was established in 1860 at a time when many village schools opened. Corpus Christi College donated land near the church for the school.[333] The rector of Newnham and Mapledurwell was the trustee and the schoolmaster or mistress had to be a member of the Church of England. The school was financed through state grants, children's pence, and donations.[334] The original school was a very simple, one-roomed structure built of brick and roofed with slates; the schoolroom measured only 20 ft by 17 ft and was not partitioned in any way (Fig. 16).[335] The initial 20 to 30 pupils

---

328 *The Villager* (July 1975, September 1980).
329 *Parl. Papers*, 1819 (224), 831.
330 *Parl. Papers*, 1835 (62), 849.
331 TNA HO 107/1681/*passim* and 41.
332 *White's Dir. Hants & IOW* (1859); NA RG9/709/*passim* and 40.
333 CCCO, LB 38/44. The land donated had previously been CCCO, CH 7: a cottage and garden with common pasture for a cow and two pigs. The cottage was dilapidated in 1841: CCCO, F/3/3/9 p.175.
334 TNA, ED21/6498, HRO, 115M87/LB1.
335 HRO, 20M65/57/1/1.

Figure 16 *The school building of 1860, taken from a contemporary drawing.*

were seated in six banks of desks facing a north wall that had two large windows and a fireplace for heating. Extensive work on the school was completed in May 1881, and the schoolroom enlarged to 33ft 6in. by 17ft 3in. but with only a curtain separating the infants from the junior class; the rooms were heated by coal-fired stoves.[336] The building was extended further in 1883 aided by a parliamentary grant of £36 18s. 0d. to provide a schoolhouse, in which Annie Smith, schoolmistress, was living in 1891.[337] The extended school is depicted on two plans drawn in 1915 (Figs 17a and 17b).[338] Numbers of pupils had increased to 42 by 1883 and to 45 by 1912 making the accommodation cramped, but some pupils had left by 1914 and numbers fell to 30–35.[339]

Pupils attended from 5 to 14 years old although some infants started at three years and a few left at twelve to assist their parents. The school was staffed by a headteacher and a monitress; the latter taught the infants. In addition, the parish clergy donated books and gave scripture, dictation and arithmetic lessons and heard the pupils read and sing.[340] However, educational standards were low and in 1873 an inspector suggested the older children could find better education in Basingstoke or Old Basing, where

336 HRO, 20M65/57/1/1.
337 HRO, 115M87/A1. Census 1891.
338 HRO, H/CA1/1/1198 & 1199 (ARC 24923–4).
339 HRO, LB2, 226–7, 238.
340 HRO, 115M87/LB1, 1.

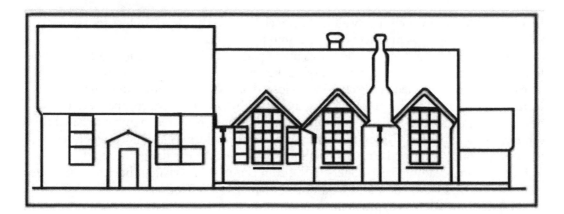

Figure 17a *The school, north elevation taken from a 1915 drawing.*

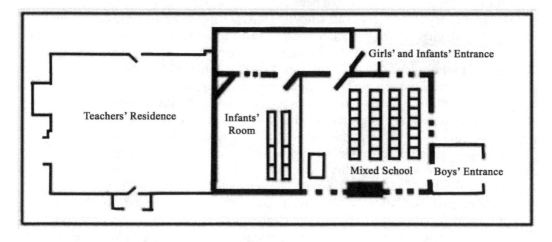

Figure 17b *The school as extended in 1883, taken from a 1915 plan.*

the schools had certificated teachers.[341] In 1883 the elder children were described as 'rather backward', although the headmistress was said to be 'careful and efficient'.[342] Low achievement was partly the result of poor attendance on account of illness, stormy weather, Basingstoke fair or the demands of the farming year. For example, in 1881 smallpox in the village caused many children to be kept away. After the five-week summer 'harvest' holiday, children frequently remained absent, assisting their parents in hop picking away from the village.[343] Attendance was particularly bad in 1891 especially

341 TNA, ED 21 6498.
342 HRO, 115M87/25.
343 HRO, 115M87/LB1 pp.3, 6; LB2, 219, 229, 236.

in Standard V from which nearly all had been absent for 100 days.[344] Closures resulting
from epidemics such as measles continued into the 20th century.[345]

Financial provision for the school was inadequate, causing the rector to gift the school
to the ratepayers in 1893 as he was out of pocket by £37 and many repairs were needed.[346]
The headteacher resigned. The school was closed for six weeks while a new management
committee comprising the principal ratepayers, led by Mr H. B. Thorp, appointed a
new certificated teacher, Miss Ada John, as head.[347] The committee members visited the
school and taught a few classes, as the rector had done before 1893. Thorp was a regular
visitor and much mourned after his death in March 1912.[348] His daughters continued to
visit the school. Leading parishioners in the 20th century who visited the school included
General and Mrs Henry Stopford Dawkins of Mapledurwell House.[349]

Despite some successes, problems continued. In June 1897 the monitress died of
diphtheria and the headmistress taught alone until September 1900.[350] The lack of
cleanliness of the pupils occasioned frequent comment from the headmistress and one
girl, whose dirty condition often had been noted, was admitted to Basingstoke Union
workhouse in May 1912.[351] As in all schools, subjects studied were partly determined
by gender, with girls studying needlework and knitting, which were examined and also
inspected from time to time by Miss Dudney and the Misses Thorp.[352] Domestic science
classes held in the village hall were not introduced for senior girls until 1932.[353] The
clergy examined religious knowledge. Apart from reading, writing and arithmetic, all
the pupils undertook nature studies which included village walks as well as practical
gardening, religious knowledge, and singing. Singing with piano accompaniment was
popular and in June 1914, 19 pupils sang at Crystal Palace in the Tonic Sol-Fa choir.[354]

The accommodation remained very poor, with appalling sanitary conditions. In
1903 the only hand washing facility was an enamelled iron basin on a wooden shelf in
the girls' cloakroom. There was no running water; water was obtained from a well on
the adjoining premises but was tainted with 'foul matter' and unfit to drink. The three
privies only 35 feet from the well were not clean, the boys' privy in particular being
'foul and dirty'. The urinal was a small brick trough, drained through a hedge; that
drain was blocked and the urinal in a dirty and offensive condition.[355] The Hampshire
county surveyor recommended the building of proper earth closets, well ventilated
and lighted.[356] In 1914 the girls' privies were described as 'dark and evil-smelling'

344   HRO, 115M87/LB2, pp.109, 145.
345   For example, HRO, 115M87/LB2, 202: the school was closed on 30 June 1911 by order of the medical
        officer for three weeks because of an outbreak of measles.
346   *Parl. Papers*, 1865 [3533]; TNA, ED21/ 6498.
347   TNA, ED 21 6498; HRO 115M87/LB1, 164–5.
348   HRO, 115M87/LB2, 212.
349   HRO, 115M87/LB3, 20, 5 November 1923. *Kelly's Dir. Hants and IOW*, 1923, 286.
350   HRO, 115M87 / LB2, 169, 218, 239, 297.
351   HRO, 115M87/ LB2, 201, 213, 220.
352   HRO, 115M87/LB2, 5, 215.
353   HRO, 115M87/ LB3, 121–22.
354   HRO, 115M87, LB2, 224, 234. Tonic Sol-Fa style avoided the need to read music.
355   TNA, ED21/6498.
356   HRO, 20M65/57/1/1; 115M67/LB3, 110.

and the approach to the school was waterlogged.[357] That year the HMI described the accommodation as 'discouraging', with the space for the infants too small to allow them to move with much freedom and the playground so small as to hardly merit the name. It was also the site of the boys' privy. A satisfactory pail closet system was installed in 1924 after the Queen's College gave the school 1/8 a. of adjoining land to extend the playground and accommodate the sanitary facilities.[358]

Early 20th century reports on the attainments of the pupils varied but increasingly highlighted low standards.[359] In 1919 the HMI commented on the 'lamentable' ignorance of the pupils, especially in elementary subjects, but a very few boys and girls did gain scholarship places at Basingstoke High School or Queen Mary's Grammar School, Basingstoke.[360] In 1924 the Director of Education for Southampton reported that Mapledurwell was a small and poor parish where only the Thorp family could afford to subscribe to the school.[361] In 1934 the newly appointed headteacher found the standard of work, especially in English, to be very poor.[362] There was an average of 34 pupils on the roll in the 1920s. Attendance was 47 in 1930, but after that it fell steadily. In 1936 there were only 28 pupils on the register, and it was reported that there was too much noise 'for diligent work', owing to the lack of separate classrooms for infants and juniors.[363] The headmistress resigned and the school closed on 8 January 1939. The older pupils transferred to Basingstoke and the younger to Old Basing, and transport was provided for the children.[364]

The School in Wartime, 1917 and 1940–3

The village and school briefly hosted evacuees during the First World War. Twenty London children from the bombed area of Walworth were admitted to the school on 25 October 1917 and returned home on 17 November. Eight children from the 'raid district of Bow' were admitted on 27 November and left on 5 December when the village was afflicted with an epidemic of scarlet fever and the school closed until the new year.[365]

In the Second World War the school, which had closed in 1939, reopened from June 1940 to 1943 as a war-time emergency school financed by Hampshire Education Committee to accommodate 25 pupils evacuated from Albert Road School, Portsmouth, as Old Basing school could not take all the refugees.[366] Two Portsmouth teachers taught the children. The school buildings were rapidly recommissioned, with whist tables used as desks. In August 1940, 30 local pupils also transferred from Old Basing school. As happened elsewhere, Portsmouth children were taught in the mornings

357 TNA, ED 21 6498 HMI report 12 June 1914; HRO 115M87/A4/1.
358 TNA, ED 21 29493.
359 For example, HRO115M87, LB3 109–10, 6 January 1931.
360 For example in July 1923, HRO, 115M87/LB3, 18.
361 TNA, ED 21/ 29493.
362 HRO, 115M87/ LB3, 146.
363 HRO, 115M87/LB3, 186.
364 HRO, 115M87LB2, 271; TNA, ED 21/6498, 52353.
365 HRO, 115M87/A1; 115M87/LB2, 258–9.
366 HRO, 115M87/LB4; H/ED1/5/243, unpaginated notes and letters.

Figure 18 *The old school and the adjoining teacher's cottage in 2012.*

and Mapledurwell children in the afternoons for a short time; full-time classes for all 50 pupils commenced at the beginning of September 1940 when four evacuees from London also joined the school.[367] Pupils were taught scripture by the rector and first aid by Miss M. Thorp who was also the school correspondent and worked in the school garden. Four of the evacuees passed the examination for the Portsmouth Secondary school.[368] Numbers fell as evacuees returned to Portsmouth from 1941: only eight Portsmouth children remained in November.[369] The school closed for the last time in September 1943 and local pupils were again transferred to Old Basing.[370] The school building was sold for domestic use in 1956 (Fig. 18), but the phases of its development are still clearly visible.[371]

In 2012 Mapledurwell primary pupils attended state schools in Old Basing and Basingstoke, while secondary pupils went to Basingstoke or Odiham, or to sixth form college in Basingstoke. However, many of the village children at both levels were privately educated. A nursery school, *The Monkey House*, established 1996, was held for a few hours each weekday in the village hall.[372]

367 HRO, 115M87/A3.
368 HRO, 115M87/A3.
369 HRO, H/ED1/5/243.
370 HRO, H/ED1/5/243.
371 TNA, ED 161/6168; BDB 12433. Change of use of schoolroom to single detached dwelling.
372 http://www.monkeyhouse.hants.sch.uk. Accessed 30 January 2011.

CHARITIES AND WELFARE

The poor of the parish benefited from private charity and parish relief from the 17th century. Smith's charity provided clothing and benefited more than half the families in the parish by 1824. Parish poor relief was at a low level in the 18th century but rose dramatically during the French wars 1793–1815. After 1834 Mapledurwell was part of Basingstoke Poor Law Union.

Smith's Charity

The only private endowed charity in Mapledurwell was created in 1678 by John Smith, then of Sherborne in Dorset but originally from Mapledurwell where he still had relatives. In 1678 he conveyed to trustees four closes of land called Bartlett's comprising 7 a. in the parish of Rotherwick, north of Newnham. Subsequent trustees always included the rector who for a long time was joined by the leading farmers of Mapledurwell.[373] The trustees were responsible for leasing the land for terms of years and for selling timber when mature. The rental money was employed for providing wool and linen clothing for the poor of Mapledurwell, with priority to any poor kin of John Smith. The trustees presented the accounts to the churchwardens each Easter.[374] In 1824 the closes were let to David Fuller on an annual tenancy of £8, and the fund also held £45 from timber sales invested at 4 per cent interest. By that time the rector was the sole trustee and the annual income was £9 16s., used to purchase linen and woollen articles at Christmas for poor parishioners who were both 'industrious and of good character', with priority to widows and aged persons. The charity was of significant value in the parish with 26 out of the 40 families receiving winter clothing in 1824.[375]

In 1894 Smith's charity was taken over by the Charity Commissioners despite opposition from the villagers and was varied by a scheme of 16 February 1932. The Charity Commission imposed conditions excluding any person in receipt of poor law relief and required that the capital was to be invested in government consuls at 2½ per cent.[376] The land was sold in 1899 to Lionel Philips of Tylney Hall, Rotherwick. In 1911 the capital amounted to £469 11s. 3d. in consols held by the official trustees; the annual income at that time was £11 14s. 8d.[377] The charity was entered on the Charity Commission register in 1965, but removed in 2004 as it had ceased to exist.[378]

---

373 *Parl. Papers* 1826 (382), 14, 400–2.

374 HRO, 49M67/PK2.

375 The closes (6a.0r.2p), were called Lower Piddle, the Long Piddle, the Little Mead and the Great Mead (1826) *Parl. Papers*, 1826 (382), 14; HRO, 49M67/PK1.

376 HRO, 49M67/PK6; www.charity-commission.gov.uk, removed charity no. 239053. Accessed 19 January 2010.

377 HRO, 50M63B97/2/4. The land was measured for sale as 8a.or.14p.

378 HRO, 35M84/382. www.charity-commission.gov.uk, no. 239053. HRO file 49M67/PK3 containing Smith's charity correspondence 1928–67 was temporarily removed by a parish official in 1988 and not returned by 2012. The Charity Commission destroyed their files after the charity had been removed for five years. Accessed 19 January 2010.

Allotments

In 1863 a 2 a. allotment to be worked by the poor was created when the commons were
inclosed. A £2 rent charge was payable by the churchwardens and overseers, and later
by the parish council, to Corpus Christi College as lords of the manor. This was to
compensate for produce lost based on the value of wheat, barley and oats in 1863. The
allotments were on the Little Moor, numbered 40 on the 1863 plan,[379] and in 2012 lay
alongside Frog Lane. They were disused from 1996 to 2008 when a new allotment society
was formed. In 2012 the allotments were managed by the parish council, both flourishing
and encouraging social activity.[380] The rent charge was due to expire in 2037 as a result of
the Rent Charges Act 1977.[381]

Poor Relief before 1834

Very few bequests to the poor were made in the 16th century, only two of wheat for
bread and two small monetary bequests (8d., 12d.).[382] One third of testators from 1600
to 1640 made such bequests, mainly of money ranging from 3s. 4d. up to 10s., though
there were also two bequests of wheat.[383] After 1640 there were few bequests, with care
for the poor by 1660 presumably being perceived as the responsibility of the overseers
of the poor and the parish rates.[384] For much of the 18th century the demands on the
poor rates were modest with, for example, £25 distributed in 1783. Rates rose rapidly
during the French Wars 1793–1815, as they did throughout England as a result of the
vastly increased food prices. In 1804 a total of £157 was collected in the poor rate and
£128 spent in comparison with £20 spent in 1776. All the payments were outdoor relief
with seven adults and their eight children receiving permanent relief and three people
relieved occasionally.[385] The increase continued with £154 and £200 raised in 1810 and
1815. Three years after the war in 1818–19, £291 was distributed which included £107
paid to 12 men for 'grubbing up wood'. This is likely to have been Upgrove woodland
which had been converted to copyhold in 1793 and was probably work creation for men
in the post-war depression. In the same account £117 was spent on bread for the poor.[386]
Expenditure eventually fell to £137 in 1825 but then rose to £219 in 1829.[387] In 1835 £159
was levied and £134 spent on the poor, while in 1837 £92 was levied and £94 spent. The
amount levied rose to £172 in 1839 before falling to £139 in 1842.[388]

---

379   HRO, 49M67/PD3.
380   http://www.mapledurwell.gov.uk/council/parish_notice_board_detail.asp?suppress_
       tools=yes&evps=39&evco= 1709. Accessed 2012.
381   Rent Charges Act 1977 (c.30).
382   HRO,1552U/59, 1580A/96, 1583B/59, 1583B/77.
383   HRO,1620A31;1632A/085;1635B/008;1637A/065;1638A;1639A/207; 1641A/010.
384   HRO, 1646A/52; TNA:PRO, PROB 11/282; HRO, 1664A/035;1686A/030.
385   *Parl. Papers*, 1803–4 (175), 453.
386   HRO, 49M67/P02.
387   *Parl. Papers*, 1830–1 (83), 178.
388   *Parl. Papers*, 1836 (595), 910, 1837 (546), 361.

Expenditure included payments for fostering of children and the aged, sickness (including coffins), food, clothing, rent, and removals to other parishes of paupers not settled in Mapledurwell.[389] In 1833 the parish vestry gained permission from Corpus Christi College to allow the poor of the parish to be employed in digging peat from 1 a. of the Great Moor where digging would not interfere with its pastoral use.[390] The following year, as a result of the Poor Law Amendment Act, care of the poor of Mapledurwell was largely transferred to the guardians of Basingstoke Union workhouse situated in Old Basing. This system continued until abolished by the Local Government Act 1929.

Settlement and Bastardy

There is very little surviving evidence of settlement issues in Mapledurwell. From 1719 to 1822 there were only five removal orders: three to the parish and two out of the parish; two settlement examinations took place and three settlement certificates were issued. This suggests stability of population with little movement in and out. In 1790 complaints were registered against John Dyke, maltster, once of Mapledurwell, for abandoning his three children who had become chargeable to the parish rates. From 1788–93 keeping Dyke's children cost the parish about £10 a year. In 1792 he was given a pauper burial, but occasional payments to his son continued in the 1790s.[391]

Medical Services

There was no medical practitioner in the village until 1932 apart from 50-year-old Amelia Harrison, who was described as a nurse in 1851.[392] However regular payments were made from the churchwardens' account to Basingstoke Cottage Hospital from 1903 to 1924 for care of parishioners.[393]

389 HRO, 49M67/PO1 & PO2.
390 CCCO, Cb 17/6.
391 HRO, 3M70/55/60; 100M71/PO2/2; 47M81/PO6/121; 3M70/56/4; 47M81/PO5/55; 19M76/PO4/44A;
      10M 57/01/2; 6M77/PO2/24; 47M81/PO3/37; 94M82/PO6/4; 44M69/G3/710; 49M67/PO2.
392 TNA, HO107/385/12: HO107/1641/41.
393 HRO, 49M67/PW2.

RELIGIOUS HISTORY

MAPLEDURWELL WAS PART of a complex and changing pattern of parishes in this part of the county. Just as the Domesday manor of Mapledurwell had been broken up into different elements, so the parochial units were sub-divided. Mapledurwell had a chapel probably by the late 12th century that was dependent on Newnham (four miles to the east).[394] It was occasionally referred to as a rectory, as it was in 1448.[395] Unusually for a chapel, by the 17th century and probably much earlier, Mapledurwell had burial, baptismal and marriage rights, although it remained a chapel until 1922 when it became an independent perpetual curacy.[396] It was, however, insufficiently endowed and it continued to be served by non-residents as part of an increasing group of ministries. The chapelry was often poorly served, and from the late 17th century there was intermittent nonconformity: first a small but influential Quaker group, and in the 19th and 20th centuries a Congregationalist group with their own chapel.

PAROCHIAL ORGANIZATION

The mother church of St Nicholas, Newnham, began as a chapel, granted by Adam de Port in the early 12th century, a time when many parishes were created, along with the tithes of Newnham and Mapledurwell to the abbey of St Vigor of Cerisy, of which Monk Sherborne priory was a cell.[397] Monk Sherborne exercised the advowson on the abbey's behalf in the 13th and 14th centuries, except in periods such as the Hundred Years War when England was at war with France, and the king of England took the right of presentation from alien priories.[398] The rector of Newnham had to pay a rent of £2 a year to the prior and convent of Monk Sherborne, who in 1387 sued William rector of Newnham for £4 arrears.[399] When the priory was suppressed as an alien house in 1462, the advowson was transferred to God's House, Southampton, but because Edward III had given God's House to the Queen's College, Oxford, the endowments and the presentment of the rectors of Newnham were transferred to the college.[400] With

---

394 For Newnham parish see the draft parish history on www.victoriacountyhistory.ac.uk/counties/hampshire (forthcoming).

395 WCM, 29922d.

396 HRO, 49M67/2/PR1.

397 H.E. Salter, *Facsimiles of Early Charters in Oxford Muniment Rooms*, (1929). M. Grant, 'The Alien Benedictine Priory of Monk Sherborne, Hampshire, from the twelfth to the fifteenth centuries', *Proc. Hants Field Club*, 55, 2000, 47.

398 For example in 1339 (*Cal. Pat.* 1338–40, 321) when John de Peueseye, was presented by Edward III.

399 *Reg. Wykeham*, ii (1899), p.593.

400 *VCH Hants*, II, 228.

few exceptions, as in 1569 and 1904–7, most of the rectors from the 17th to the 19th centuries were selected from fellows of the Queen's College who had been born in the north of England, including some very long serving clergy such as Dr Joseph Richmond of Crosby, Cumberland, who was rector from 1762 until his death at the age of 98 in 1816.[401] By contrast, when curates were appointed they were generally not from the Queen's College: thus John W. Corbet, curate of Newnham cum Mapledurwell from 1876, was from St John's College, Cambridge, and Revd S. E. Terry, appointed curate of Mapledurwell in 1888, was from St Alban Hall, Oxford.[402] A very few rectors, such as Charles H. C. Baker in 1900, from St Edmund Hall, Oxford, were not ex-fellows of the Queen's College.[403] Although the college continued to be patron of the Newnham rectory in the 20th century, amalgamations of local parishes meant that presentations had to be shared with others such as Lord Dorchester and briefly the bishop of Winchester.[404] From 1886 Newnham also had a dependent chapel in neighbouring Hook.[405]

Endowment

The tithes and glebe of Newnham and Mapledurwell were the property of the rector, who used some of the issues to finance a curate. In 1838, the tithes of Newnham were valued at £305 and those of Mapledurwell at £220 a year. There were almost 29 a. of glebe in Newnham and 9 a. in Mapledurwell which, until the inclosure of 1797, were dispersed in the common fields. Newnham glebe included a parsonage house, garden and barn. In Mapledurwell by 1616 (and possibly earlier) the rector owned Glebe Cottage (Fig. 19) with an orchard and barn adjoining the main street.[406] Following the inclosure of 1797 the allocated glebe was named Parsonage field and comprised 9 a. of arable land in Down field separated from the rector's barn and orchard by the Little Common Moor.[407] All the glebe land and property was leased by 1841.[408] No tithe was collected in kind in 1838 but the parsonage barn remained until it was dismantled and its brick, timber, and thatch sold in 1854.[409] In 1873 the benefice of Mapledurwell, described as a perpetual curacy, was valued at £213 with that of Newnham, described as a rectory, valued at £262.[410]

401   HRO, 21M65A1/26. Last presentation before transfer 10 Feb 1901. Return of Transfers of rights of Patronage under the Benefice Act 1898; HRO, 49M67/PW10; *Parson and Parish*, 202; *Doing the Duty*, 83.
402   *Crockford Clerical Dir.* (1889), 1235
403   *Crockford Clerical Dir.* (1903), 57.
404   For example, *Crockford Clerical Dir.* (1967–8), 1670, recorded the Queens College three turns, Lord Dorchester one turn.
405   *VCH Hants*, iv, 158.
406   CCCO, Langdon Map MS 532/2/11. HRO 21M65/F7/152/1–2; 10M57/C117.
407   HRO, Q23/2/80.
408   HRO, 21M65/F7/152/1–2.
409   HRO, 10M57/C117.
410   *Parl. Papers*, 1873 [C.856].

Figure 19 *Glebe Cottage.*

The Chapelry of Mapledurwell

Architectural evidence suggests that the present church, dedicated to St Mary, was built at the end of the 12th or beginning of the 13th century, although it may have been built before 1233 when a lease granted land south of the chapel of Mapledurwell.[411] The rector of Newnham was responsible for serving the chapel but at times failed to do so adequately. Baptismal and burial registers survive from 1616 and marriage registers from 1666, and the chapelry also had its own churchwardens. In 1838 separate tithe settlements were made with the rector for Newnham and for Mapledurwell.[412] In 1873 Newnham rectory and Mapledurwell perpetual curacy were reported to be 'held together.'[413]

411 TNA, E 40/3242. Agreement between Theobald,the abbot, and the convent of Tyron (Andwell), and Alan Basset. They released to Alan all claim in Hoc (Hook) wood and give him land in the field 'del su' of the chapel of 'Mapeldurewelle'. (Morrow of the nativity of St John the Baptist, AD 1223). S. Himsworth, *Winchester College Muniments*, i (1976),109.

412 TNA:PRO, IR 18 9082, 9062.

413 *Parl. Papers*, 1873 [C.856] Report of the commissioners appointed to enquire into the property and income of the universities of Oxford and Cambridge, page image 622.

Parochial Reorganisation since 1918

Mapledurwell was officially separated from the benefice of Newnham in 1922 and made an independent perpetual curacy.[414] The rector of Newnham retained half of the value of the tithe rent-charge of Mapledurwell, which had risen to £230, so only £118 remained to endow the new perpetual curacy.[415] That income was insufficient to enable a full-time curate to be employed, so the vicar of Basing, who also held Up Nately vicarage, was authorised to hold the perpetual curacy of Mapledurwell in plurality.[416] The parishioners unsuccessfully petitioned Edward Talbot, bishop of Winchester, for restoration of the tithes. When Corpus Christi and Winchester Colleges were asked to contribute towards the church expenses in 1925, Winchester College sent £3 but Corpus Christi apparently sent nothing.[417] Although parishioners opposed proposals for further unions of parishes in the 1930s, the rectors from 1935 to 1956 were appointed to Newnham St Nicholas with Hook, Nately Scures, Mapledurwell, Andwell, and Rotherwick with the tithes of Mapledurwell restored to the rector of Newnham.[418] The grouping was subsequently divided with Mapledurwell forming a separate parish with Newnham, Nately Scures and Up Nately.[419] Greywell was added to these in 1984 to form a new parish which continued in 2012.[420] In 2008 this group of parishes joined the Herriard Benefice (Herriard, Weston Patrick, Upton Grey, Tunworth, Long Sutton, South Warnborough) with the parish of Odiham to form the North Hampshire Downs Benefice, which is led by the rector who in 2012 lived in Upton Grey rectory. Mapledurwell retained a priest in charge.[421]

PASTORAL CARE AND RELIGIOUS LIFE

The annexation of Mapledurwell to the rectory of Newnham from the Middle Ages until 1922 and the many parochial amalgamations after that date often led to disputes over whether the cure of souls in Mapledurwell was adequately served. At times it had a dedicated resident curate but this was far from a permanent provision.

The Middle Ages to the Reformation

There was a chantry chapel within Mapledurwell church from the late 13th century, established and endowed with land worth £5 a year by Ela in 1290 after the death of her second husband, Philip Basset.[422] She gave land to the bishop of Winchester, John

---

414 By Order in Council, 4 June 1918.
415 TNA, IR 18/9062.
416 CE Rec. Centre, NB41/139B.
417 HRO, 49M67/PP1, Parochial Church Council minutes 1920–58, unpaginated.
418 *Crockford Clerical Dir.* (1937), 1713. CE Rec. Centre, N3372, 24 .12.1936.
419 CE Rec. Centre, NB41/139/B. Order in Council, *The London Gazette*, 10 May 1955.
420 http://www.mapledurwell.gov.uk/churches. Accessed 30 March 2011.
421 http://www.mapledurwell.gov.uk/churches/default.asp. Accessed 14 July 2012.
422 Himsworth, *Winchester College Muniments*, ii. (1984), 110. Ela, dau. of Wm de *Longespée*, earl of Salisbury, was previously married to Thomas Newburgh, earl of Warwick. She was still described as

of Pontoise and his successors, to provide a chaplain in the chapel, with the right of presentation. On Ela's death, Alan Plunkenet became lord of the manor for life and appointed Robert de Northampton as chaplain; the bishops regained the right to appoint the chaplain after an enquiry in 1314.[423] In 1323 Adam de Rodebroke was canonically inducted as chantry chaplain and the chantry was still listed as worth £5 a year in a list drawn up between 1333 and 1345.[424] After that the chantry appears to have fallen into disuse as there is no further record of the appointment of a chaplain and the chantry is not listed in the chantry certificates for the diocese of Winchester of 1546 and 1548.[425]

One long-standing concern was neglect of the congregation, as in 1454 when Mapledurwell's inhabitants complained that the rector, William Boswell, had failed to hold services as agreed. The rector was ordered to hold services himself or to employ a chaplain, and to keep the chancel in repair under pain of a 3s. 4d. fine for each default.[426] Nevertheless his successor in 1515 (William Eastwood) was still failing to provide a chaplain. The bishop's commissary accepted the churchwardens' and inhabitants' view that the rector took enough from the 'fertile vill in rents and oblations' to support one, and judgement against the rector was confirmed by Bishop Fox.[427]

The national religious tensions of the early 16th century were evident in the parish. One rector, Richard Fetherston MA (1520–21) later became a prominent Catholic martyr by opposing the royal divorce and Henry VIII's assumption of the title of supreme head of the church: Fetherston was executed in 1540.[428] In Mapledurwell all surviving wills from 1518 to 1547, before the Edwardian Reformation, upheld traditional Catholic views, revealing a religiously conservative population who bequeathed their souls to Almighty God, our Lady Saint Mary and all the Holy Company of Heaven.[429] The will of Thomas Wylde (1552) continued this tradition into Edward VI's reign, leaving his soul to Our Lady St Mary and requesting four masses at his burial and 'monthe mynd'.[430] All other testators under Edward VI and Elizabeth showed the influence of the Protestant Reformation in leaving their souls to Almighty God alone: Robert Fry in 1571 left his soul to Almighty God beseeching him to receive it to Abraham's bosom as he did for Lazarus.[431]

In the early 16th century many wills made small bequests to the cathedral church in Winchester and to the parish church of Mapledurwell.[432] Two sheep were bequeathed in 1518 and in 1545 Agnes Kinge, widow and member of a wealthy family, left 2d. to

---

countess of Warwick.

423 *Regs. Sandale & Asser*, 142–6.
424 *ibid.* 515. *VCH Hants*, IV, 152. 'Appendix 1 to the Wickham Register' in *Reg. Wykeham*, i(1896–9), XI, 362.
425 TNA; PRO, E301/51 and 52.
426 CCCO, MS C 6 cap 13 (1), 2.
427 CCCO, MS C 6 cap 13 (1), 19.
428 E.H. Shagan, 'Fetherston, Richard (d.1540)', *ODNB* (2004) http://www.oxforddnb.com/view/article9374. Accessed 12 July 2012.
429 For example, HRO, 1545B/140.
430 HRO, 1552U/69.
431 HRO, 1571 B/069.
432 HRO, 1518B/39, 1545B/92, 1571B/69/1.

Winchester cathedral and one cow to maintain a taper for the Holy Sacrament.[433] Leading figures in Basingstoke occasionally gave money to support churches in the hundred, as did John Ronagar, alderman, who in 1558 left 3s. 4d. to Mapledurwell church.[434]

The Reformation to 1800

In the 16th and early 17th centuries pastoral provision appeared to be much improved with a series of resident curates ministering to their spiritual needs. All surviving Mapledurwell wills between 1518 and 1580 were witnessed by a member of the parish clergy, usually the curate.[435] The curates were John Lancaster, Raffe Colmar, William Drake, Thomas Pearson, and John Turner;[436] the appointments of John Fycas (1551), Richard Powell (1579), Robert Holmes (1680), Mr Beaton (1691) were also recorded.[437] The death in 1630 of Henry Dyer, 'Clerk and curat' of Mapledurwell, is recorded in the burial register.[438] Those curates apparently inhabited Glebe Cottage in The Street and had a parsonage barn for storing the rector's tithes. In 1616 Glebe Cottage was recorded as the parsonage. The 16th or 17th century two-storey thatched cottage survived in 2012.[439]

Adherence to the established church continued in the 17th century. In 1603 there were 80 communicants. There were no Roman Catholics or non-communicants.[440] There is some evidence of Laudian innovation in the 1630s: churchwardens' accounts for 1635 included 'For cloth to make the surplice 20s', and in 1637 the churchwardens spent 27s. on the Communion table and rails.[441] There are no accounts from 1637 to 1650, but in 1652 the church inventory comprised 'the pulpit cloth and the cushion with a linen table cloth. Item the church book with a flagon and a silver bowl with the cover and a basket'.[442]

No rector or curate was deprived during the Commonwealth or at the Restoration, although glebe land (9½ a. in the common fields) and a cottage were let by the Queen's College in 1658 to John Sumner, freeholder and yeoman, rather than to the rector. Sumner gave a bond for £50 which was forfeitable if he did not pay the rent: Andrew Whelpdale, fellow of the Queen's College at least until 1658 and rector of Newnham with Mapledurwell from 1663, witnessed the bond.[443]

---

433 HRO, 1543B/065, 1545B/92.
434 Baigent and Millard, *Basingstoke*, 32.
435 See, for example, HRO 1518B/39.
436 HRO, 1518B/39; 1543B/06; 1545B/09; 1545B/140; 1547B/05; 1551U/092; 1552U/59; 1552U/69; 1566A/52; 1571B/069;1580A/83; 1580A/96.
437 Clergy of the Church of England database. http://www.theclergydatabase.org.uk. Accessed 30 March 2011. The Lancasters were a family of wealthy merchants in Basingstoke.
438 HRO, 49M67/2/PR1.
439 CCCO MS 532/2/11; *Hampshire Treasures*, 2 (2006), 181.
440 *Dioc. Pop. Rtns*, 490.
441 Below, Religious Buildings.
442 HRO, 49M67/PR1.
443 The Queen's Coll. Mun., Mapledurwell, A1, A4. No evictions listed in *Calamy Revised*, nor in *Walker Revised*.

In the 1660s, Whelpdale appears to have found it difficult to find a reliable curate for Mapledurwell and was forced to keep the Mapledurwell registers himself, complaining that

> for want of A Better Booke I was forced to Register things as well as I could in this, and as my parishioners desired; the Curates I employed being too negligent with the performance of this Duty But from the yeare 1666 I began myselfe to take Care both of the Christening Marriages and Burials and Registered them in that Booke the Churchwardens keepe, as Appears in the said Booke.[444]

Such neglect may have contributed to the emergence of small-scale non-conformity by the 1670s. The Compton Census of 1676 recorded 70 conformists and 6 nonconformists.[445] The Smith family of Quakers was influential locally and in 1680 churchwardens presented: 'Roger Smith senior and Roger Smith junior Alice Smith his daughter deputed Quakers for not comeing Church nor receiving Sacrament'.[446] In 1684 Roger Smith senior requested 'my body to bee buried at Alton in the said County in the buriall place of the people called Quakers'.[447] The Quaker meeting house in Alton was built in 1672 and was still a centre of worship in 2012.[448] Smith, farmer of the second biggest Corpus Christi College copyhold (The Farm) and a maltster, was worth £713 at his death.[449]

Smith's son, also Roger and a Quaker, inherited the copyhold but was imprisoned for 12 days at Basingstoke for non payment of tithes, then carried to Winchester gaol whence he was removed to London.[450] Roger Smith the younger died in 1689 leaving his sister Alice as reversioner though her religion proved problematic.[451] In 1690 William Hall, Corpus Christi College bailiff, recorded that Alice

> is not willing to fill up her Coppy because she hath none to put in and she says next year she hopes she may have a child of her own for I know that her marriage writings are sealed, only I think she is ashamed to be married, he being a churchman and not above ½ her age.[452]

Alice did marry John Pitman but William Hall continued to find her an unsatisfactory tenant, dismissing her as 'fickle and impertinent' and attributing both to her sex and 'chiefly her religion'.[453] Alice Pitman died in 1692, after which there is no evidence of

---

444 HRO, 49M67/PR1.
445 *Compton Census*, 84.
446 HRO, 202M85/3/773.
447 TNA, Roger Smith PROB 11/378 1684.
448 http://www.altonquakers.org.uk/altonquakers-his.html. Accessed 30 March 2011.
449 CCCO, CH 11; TNA:PRO PROB 4/8604.
450 Besse, *Sufferings*, 240. (Reference supplied by Rosalind Johnson).
451 CCCO, Newlyn Correspondence, 30 June 1689.
452 CCCO, Newlyn correspondence, 1690.
453 CCCO, Newlyn correspondence, 1690, F/3/3/4, 54.

Quakers in the village.[454] There was only one nonconformist in 1725 and none in 1765–88.[455]

Provision of a curate in the 18th century was intermittent.[456] In 1725 the rector of Newnham, Michael Hutchinson, had a curate called Thomas Skelton and one or other of them read prayers and preached in Mapledurwell each Sunday afternoon.[457] In 1736 John Lowry was appointed curate.[458] Although no curate held office in 1765, services were held on Sunday evenings.[459] In 1772 there was still accommodation for the curate in the glebe, with a house and garden, barn and 1 a. piddle adjoining; the churchyard was a ¼a.[460]

From 1800 to 1922

The congregation retained its traditionalism, petitioning against Catholic emancipation in 1829.[461] In 1810 the church could accommodate a congregation of 100 people.[462] In 1851 there were 15 free sitting places and 98 unfree; 75 attended church on 1 March with an average attendance of 80 declared.[463] The building underwent major restoration from 1850 to 1854, when the pews were altered to provide an additional 15 free places for the poor and a vestry was built.[464] The £231 cost was met by the Diocesan Society, church rates, subscriptions and the Incorporated Church Building Society. The last of these had been established in 1818 to support the enlargement, building, and repair of Anglican churches and chapels.[465] Corpus Christi College and its copyholder tenants granted 29 perches of land in 1869 to extend the graveyard.[466]

In the early 19th century there was a resident curate, but that arrangement ceased later in the century to the detriment of local worship. John Lewis, a licensed curate, was appointed in 1816 with a salary of £100, surplice fees, and the glebe cottage with the garden and meadow.[467] However, in 1832 when John Hodgson became stipendiary curate of Newnham, the stipend of £75 was increased by £15 in lieu of the glebe house;[468] Thomas B. Thompson was similarly appointed in 1835.[469] Rectors of Newnham then

454 CCCO, F/3/3/4, p.77.
455 *Parson and Parish*, 202, 304.
456 HRO, 21M65 A2/4, E6/1.
457 *Parson and Parish*, 96; HRO, 21M65/F1/11.
458 HRO, 21M65/B1/76.
459 *Parson and Parish*, 202.
460 HRO, 35M48/16/293, J. Richmond, rector, 4 June 1772.
461 *Parl. Papers*, 1829; House of Lords Journal, vol. 6, 1829.
462 *Doing the Duty*, 12, note 4.
463 *Rel. Census 1851*, 179.
464 Below, The Church of St Mary.
465 LPL Church plans. Mapledurwell, Application 4289. The architect was Benjamin Thorne of Basingstoke. Divine services during restoration were held at Up Nately.
466 CE Rec. Centre, ECE/7/1/ 41275.
467 HRO, 21M65/E7/1/136; 21M65A2/4.
468 HRO, 21 M65 E6/1.
469 HRO, 21M65 E6/1.

rented out the cottage and the glebe for agricultural use.[470] In 1881 the curate lived in a cottage in Newnham,[471] and Mapledurwell parishioners suffered, as shown in 1893 when the rector felt unable to supervise the National school as he lived four miles away. The leading farmers were reported to be 'at loggerheads with the rector'.[472]

Nonconformity from 1850

Nonconformity reappeared in the village from the middle of the 19th century.[473] By 1851 there was an Independent or Congregationalist group that attracted an average of 70 worshippers. The Independents met in a building erected before 1800, which was not used solely for its services. The preacher was Charles Othen, of Hackwood Road, Basingstoke.[474] In 1867 five dissenting families were recorded.[475] A purpose-built Congregational chapel to accommodate 90 persons was erected in 1864 by Joseph Addison at a cost of £130 on his Winchester College copyhold land that lay on the main village street immediately north of his freehold, Webbs Farm.[476] Although the chapel was built on his land, there is no evidence that Addison himself attended or supported the chapel.[477] By the turn of the 20th century that chapel was one of seven village chapels overseen by an evangelist attached to London Street Congregational church, Basingstoke.[478] Leading members of the chapel were the family of Thomas Kingdom, a prosperous ironmonger who worked in Basingstoke and lived in Mapledurwell.[479] In 1906 the Hampshire Congregational Union reported a range of activities in Mapledurwell additional to their Sunday services: 'Mothers' Meeting every Monday, at which a Gospel Address is given by the Evangelist, Band of Hope, and a weekly Preaching service during the winter months.' There was also a Sunday school.[480] Some pupils from the village school were Congregationalists and school closed early on a number of occasions at that period to allow the children to attend tea at the chapel. Miss Mabel Thorp presented prizes for the Band of Hope examination.[481] However, the chapel had inadequate support and from the First World War until 1929 it was 'temporarily closed'.[482] Although *Hampshire Treasures* states that the chapel was 'last used for worship'

---

470   HRO, 21M65/F7/152/1-2; 21M65/E2/650; TNA, HO 107/1681/40; RG 9/709/39A; RG10 1235/77; RG11 1255/68; RG12 958/90; RG13 1109/36.

471   TNA, RG11 1255.

472   TNA, ED 21, 6498.

473   Roger Ottewill researched and wrote the text on Mapledurwell Congregational Chapel.

474   *Religious Census 1851*, 179; *Hampshire Treasures*, 2 184.

475   *Parl. Papers*, 1867 [3840].

476   WCM, 21309; *White's Dir. Hants* (1878), 322; *Hampshire Treasures*, 2. 184. OS Map, 1:10560, sheet XIX (1871 edn); *VCH Hants*, IV, 149; Unreferenced letter from Paul Addison to Winchester College, WCM, 2 June 1894.

477   WCM, letter Paul Addison, 2 June 1894.

478   The other chapels were at Cuffaude, Ellisfield, Farleigh, Pyotts Hill, Winslade and Worting.

479   *Basingstoke Congregational Magazine*, new series, Vol. 1 (January 1908).

480   Annual Report of HCU 1906, HRO 127M94/62/51.

481   HRO, 115M87/LB 1&2. 216.

482   For example, HRO, 127M94/62/62, Annual Report of HCU 1918. The copyhold appears to have been converted to a leasehold by 1894 when P. Addison offered the college £12 p.a. for a 21-year lease for the

in 1930,[483] London Street Congregational church recorded indirectly that the chapel had served as a place of worship on a regular basis throughout the 1930s. Indeed, there were a number of positive developments; for example, in 1935 it was reported that 20 young people were attending evening service which augured well for the future, and in 1937, 'some of … [the] preachers going out to Mapledurwell [from Basingstoke]… met with encouragement in somewhat larger numbers to welcome them.' It was also possible for the chapel to support a separate Women's Meeting.[484]

Nevertheless by 1939 attendance had declined to such an extent that the London Street deacons decided that the chapel should be closed. In 1944, London Street received the chapel as a bequest from the owner, the late Paul Addison, who in 1926 had bought the 2½ a. of land on which the chapel was built from Winchester College for £350.[485] The deacons agreed 'that the building should be accepted as a gift, provided there was no question of the re-opening of the chapel.'[486] It was later much altered and in 2012 was a house called The Old Chapel.

Religious Life since 1922

From 1922 Mapledurwell was served with Up Nately by the vicar of Basing.[487] A parochial church council replaced the vestry in 1922.[488] From 1935 to 1956 a new amalgamation meant that one rector served eight churches and resided in Hook rectory.[489] This diminished his effectiveness in Mapledurwell, and in 1947 a special episcopal visitation invited all the churchwardens to Winchester, with the main discussion focussing on raising attendance by holding services in rotation in the united churches.[490] In 1951 at the parochial church council, the rector apologised for not visiting Mapledurwell as often as he would like and spoke of the difficulties of the clergy. Similarly, in 1953 the new rector, the Revd R. A. Dacre, reflected on the problems of finance and the lack of assistance.[491] A number of curates were appointed in the first half of the 20th century but only one, Revd A. H. Lunn (1937), had specific responsibility for Mapledurwell (combined with Nately Scures);[492] he probably lived in Nately Scures rectory as did the Revd G. D. Hills-Harrop, curate of Newnham with Nately Scures from 1952.[493] After Hook, Greywell and Rotherwick formed a separate parish in 1955, the vicar of Newnham, Mapledurwell, Nately Scures and Up Nately took up residence in Nately

---

small piece of land which included the site of the chapel.

483 *Hampshire Treasures*, 2, 184.

484 Records of London Street Congregational church, Basingstoke; *Basingstoke and District Congregational Magazine*, 30, no. 11, New Series, November 1937, 9.

485 WCM, uncatalogued 20th century documents relating to Mapledurwell. Conveyance, 26 April 1926.

486 *London Street Congregational Church Deacons' Meeting Minutes*, 24 April 1944, 315.

487 *Crockford Clerical Dir.* (1926), 1875.

488 HRO, 49M67/PW11.

489 Above, Parochial Reorganisation since 1918.

490 HRO, 49M 67/PW9, 10, 11.

491 *Crockford Clerical Dir.* (1953–4), 1597; HRO 49 M 67/ PP1.

492 *Crockford Clerical Dir.* (1937), 841.

493 *Crockford Clerical Dir.* (1952), 542.

Scures rectory.[494] During the first half of the 20th century the owners of Mapledurwell House played an increasing role in the parish, acting as rector's churchwarden, and hosted parochial church council meetings rather than using the church.[495]

Many improvements were made to the church. In 1909 an organ was purchased at a cost of £120. Corpus Christi College donated ¼ a. on the north side to extend the churchyard. In 1957 electricity was installed in the church. In 1959–60 there was considerable work to install new heating, lighting and to treat death-watch beetle. Corpus Christi College contributed £5 towards eradicating the death-watch beetle, for which, and also treating wet rot, the cost was £233 17s. Repairs to the east window in 1967, including removing and restoring the leaded lights, cost £149.

Since 1984, when St Mary's Mapledurwell has been part of a united parish with Newnham, Nately Scures, Up Nately and Greywell, the vicar has lived in Up Nately Rectory within the combined civil parish of Mapledurwell and Up Nately. In 2008 Revd Jane Leese was the first woman to be appointed vicar of the parish. In 2012 the church was open and well maintained, with communion services or family services most Sundays. The church was quite wealthy, with the friends' organisation responsible for raising funds.

THE CHURCH OF ST MARY

The church of St Mary is built on a small rise on the southern edge of the village (Fig. 20). It consists of a small single cell nave with projecting chancel, altogether about 50 feet long. A small vestry was added in the 19th century on the south side of the chancel, and there is a wooden, timber clad bell-tower inset into the west end of the nave. The church is built of dressed and plain flint externally with dressed masonry, originally clunch, in the quoins and window and door surrounds. These were heavily restored in the 19th century.[496] Before these restorations the walls were described as being of rough flints and mortar.[497] There is little obvious diagnostic material for dating and the early details have generally been replaced by the heavy 19th century work. The six small nave windows and a window in the north wall of the chancel all probably possess original interior openings but with distinct rebuilt upper parts. The latter, with their simple slightly pointed heads, suggest that the building had been constructed by about 1200 and that it was the chapel first documented in 1233.[498] The grant of the tithes of Mapledurwell with the tithes and chapel of Newnham, confirmed in 1154–72, suggest that the chapel did not then exist.[499]

The church has gone through three major periods of change, although none has altered the original size or plan. The building was dramatically changed in the second half of the 15th and early 16th century. The fine nave roof, with its tie beams, curved braced collars and two rows of butt purlins, suggests that it was a replacement in the

494 *Crockford Clerical Dir.* (1955–6), 296.
495 HRO, 49 M 67/ PP1.
496 Accounts provided in *VCH Hants*, IV, 152. *Pevsner North Hampshire*, 388.
497 LPL, ICBS, 4289
498 S. Himsworth, *Winchester College Muniments*, II (1984), 160–1.
499 H.E.Salter, *Facsimiles of Early Charters in Oxford Muniment Rooms* (1929), 21.

Figure 20 *St Mary's church, from the west.*

Figure 21 *The Canner brass in Mapledurwell church.*

second half of the 15th century.[500] The timbers for the substantial bell tower, inserted at the west end of the church, have been shown by dendrochronology to have had a probable felling, and thus construction, date of 1490–1522.[501] The west door, probably made of narrow grained Baltic oak, is also of a style that suggests it is similar in date.[502] Reused fragments of carved timber in the chancel screen may also belong to that period. An early 16th-century memorial brass (Fig. 21) commemorates John Canner, one of the main figures in the village, and his wife, Agnes.[503] The earliest of the church bells was of London manufacture and is probably early 15th century.[504] Taken together, the features suggest the 15th to the early 16th centuries were a period of particular activity in this little country church.

A second phase of remodelling is reflected in the incomplete churchwardens' accounts and in surviving fragments, both of which suggest activity at the beginning of the 17th century. Timber and tiles were bought and masons employed. A new bell 'Richard Eldridge made me 1620' was acquired and brought from Wokingham, and hung in 1620.[505] A stone block with the date 1625 suggests more substantial alterations, perhaps involving the former east window, now lost through Victorian improvements. Were such alterations associated with a new window that survived at the beginning of the 19th century when the church was described as 'remarkable for its eastern window, which contains the ten commandments in stained glass'?[506] Finally, a set of altar rails were added in 1637.[507] Much of the current timber furnishings are 19th-century, as is the pulpit, although its use of Jacobean motifs may suggest the prevalence of these in the furniture and fittings that were then being replaced; some 17th-century material may be included in the 19th-century screen.

Although the building underwent major restorations, there was no significant enlargement; it was a subordinate chapel, without any significant demographic pressure or a lord or rector with pretensions of grandeur. *White's Directory* records that restoration work was carried out on the church in 1830, but it is not known what was done.[508] In 1850–4 Benjamin Thorne of Basingstoke and the Revd Wylie carried out a new phase of restoration at a proposed cost of £231.[509] The proposals to the Church Building Society list roof repairs, casing external walls, new windows in the north, south and east walls,

---

500 Edward Roberts personal communication for the information based on comparison with secular buildings dated using dendrochronology; see also E. Roberts, 'Early roofs in Hampshire' in J. Walker (ed.), *The English Medieval Roof: Crownpost to Kingpost* (2011), 60.

501 Dendrochronological dating by Dr Martin Bridge of the Oxford Dendrochronlogy Laboratory (Report 2012/20), funded by the Friends of Mapledurwell Church, the Hampshire Building Survey Group, and the Historic Buildings section of the Hampshire Field Club. To be published in *Vernacular Architecture* (2012, forthcoming).

502 Martin Bridge, personal communication.

503 On the Canner family, above: Landownership: The Major Freeholder.

504 W.E. Colchester, *Hampshire Church Bells*, (1920, reprinted 1979).

505 HRO, 49M96/PR1, see also Colchester, *Church Bells* 41, 89.

506 W. Bingley, *Collections for the History of Hampshire*, 1807–13 (HRO, 16M79/2).

507 HRO, 49M96/PR1.

508 W. White, *History, Gazetteer and Directory of Hampshire and the Isle of Wight* (1859); the earlier work is also referred to in LPL, ICBS, 4289.

509 LPL, ICBS, 4289 Proposal form/14. ICBS http://www.churchplansonline.org (accessed 28 July 2012) gives the date as 1850–1854; Pevsner *et al* (2010) give 1853.

a new vestry, and rebuilding of the tower. Inside, the walls were to be re-plastered, the stonework of the interior was to be restored and made good, the ceiling was to be taken down and the timbers repaired, the screen and the chancel communion rail were to be restored, and a new font enclosed. An ancient porch was also to be taken down.[510] Most of the works were carried out and can be seen in the effect on the appearance of the fabric, but fortunately nothing came of the proposed removal of the bell tower and erection of a replacement in the centre of the church. Wiser counsels and the weight of the bells prevailed.[511] The building was given new pews, with free seats for the poor squeezed in at the back.[512] That decoration was included in the 19th-century changes is suggested by the diaper pattern incised in the plaster lower parts of the east wall to take a colour scheme. The bells, of 1373–1418, 1620, and 1659, were repaired and re-hung in 1938, and the churchyard was extended in 1939.[513]

510 LPL, ICBS 4289 (proposals).
511 LPL, ICBS 4289 (letter from Revd G. Wylie, 13 October 1854).
512 See the plan http://www.churchplansonline.org (accessed 28 July 2012); or LPL ICBS, 4289.
513 W. E. Colchester, *Hampshire Church Bells*, 89; HRO, 49M67/PP1, unpaginated parochial church council minutes 1920–58.

ABBREVIATIONS

Abbreviations and short titles used include the following:

a.	acre(s)
Acts of PC	*Acts of the Privy Council of England* (HMSO, 1890–1964)
Archaeol. Jnl	*Archaeological Journal*
Baigent and Millard, *Basingstoke*	F.J. Baigent and J.E. Millard, *A History of the Ancient Town and Manor of Basingstoke in the County of Southampton with a Brief Account of the Siege of Basing House, A.D. 1643–1645* (Basingstoke, 1889)
Besse, *Sufferings*	J.Besse, *A Collection of the Sufferings of the People called Quakers, from 1650 to 1689* (London, 1753)
BL	British Library
Calamy Revised	A.G. Matthews (ed.), *Calamy Revised* (Oxford, 1934)
Cal. Chart	*Calendar of the Charter Rolls preserved in the Public Record Office* (HMSO, 1903–27)
Cal. Close	*Calendar of the Close Rolls preserved in the Public Record Office* (HMSO, 1892–1963)
Cal. Cttee for Compounding	*Calendar of the Proceedings of the Committee for Compounding, etc* (HMSO, 1889–92)
Cal. Cttee for Money	*Calendar of the Proceedings of the Committee for Advance of Money 1642–56* (HMSO, 1888)
Cal. Fine	*Calendar of the Fine Rolls preserved in the Public Record Office* (HMSO, 1911–62)
Cal. Inq. Misc	*Calendar of Inquisitions Miscellaneous (Chancery) preserved in the Public Record Office* (HMSO, 1916–68)
Cal. Inq. p.m	*Calendar of Inquisitions post mortem preserved in the Public Record Office* (HMSO, 1904–87)
Cal. Inq. p.m. Hen. VII	*Calendar of Inquisitions post mortem, Henry VII* (HMSO, 1898–1955)
Cal. Pat.	*Calendar of the Patent Rolls preserved in the Public Record Office* (HMSO, 1890–1986)

Cal. SP Dom.	*Calendar of State Papers, Domestic Series* (HMSO, 1856–1972)
Cat. Ancient Deeds	*Descriptive Catalogue of Ancient Deeds in the Public Record Office* (HMSO, 1890–1915)
Cath. Rec. Soc.	Catholic Record Society
CCCO	Corpus Christi College, Oxford
CE Rec. Centre	Church of England Record Centre, South Bermondsey, London
CH	Copyhold
Char. Com.	Charity Commission
Char. Don	*Abstract of Returns relative to Charitable Donations for the Benefit of Poor Persons* (Parl. Papers 1816 (511), xvi)
CJ	*Journals of the House of Commons*
Close	*Close Rolls of the Reign of Henry III preserved in the Public Record Office* (HMSO, 1902–15)
Complete Baronetage	G. E. C[okayne], *Complete Baronetage* (Exeter, 1900–9)
Complete Peerage	G. E. C[okayne] and others, *The Complete Peerage* (2nd edn 1910–59)
Compton Census	A. Whiteman (ed.), *The Compton Census of 1676* (Records of Social and Economic History, n.s. 10, 1986)
Crockford Clerical Dir.	*Crockford's Clerical Directory*
Dioc. Pop. Rtns	A. Dyer and D.M. Palliser (eds), *Diocesan Population Returns for 1563 and 1603*, (Records of Social and Economic History, n.s. 31, 2005)
Doing the Duty	Mark Smith (ed.), *Doing the Duty of the Parish: Surveys of the Church in Hampshire 1810* (HRS 17, 2004)
Excerpta e Rot. Fin	*Excerpta e Rotulis Finium*, Hen. III (Record Commission, 1835-6)
Feudal Aids	*Inquisitions and Assessments relating to Feudal Aids preserved in the Public Record Office* (HMSO, 1899-1920)
Gen. NS	*The Genealogist*, new series
HCC	Hampshire County Council
HCU	Hampshire Congregational Union
Hampshire Treasures, 2	*Hampshire Treasures Survey*, Vol. 2 Basingstoke and Deane, HCC, 1979.
Ha.	hectare(s)
Hearth Tax	Elizabeth Hughes and Philippa White (eds), *The Hampshire Hearth Tax Assessment 1665* (HRS, 11, (1991)

HER	Historic Environment Record
HRO	Hampshire Record Office
HRS	Hampshire Record Series
LPL	Lambeth Palace Library, London
m.	metre(s)
Mun.	Muniments
OS	Ordnance Survey
OS ABRC	OS Archaeology Branch Record Cards
Parl. Papers	*Parliamentary Papers*
Parson and Parish	W.R. Ward (ed.), *Parson and Parish in Eighteenth-Century Hampshire: Replies to Bishops' Visitations* (HRS 13, 1995)
Pevsner North Hampshire	Michael Bullen, John Crook, Rodney Hubbuck and Nikolaus Pevsner (eds.), *The Buildings of England. Hampshire: Winchester and the North* (London, 2010)
Plac. de Quo Warr	*Placita de Quo Warranto* (Record Commission, 1818)
PRO	The Public Record Office, now The National Archives
PRS	Pipe Roll Society
Queen's Coll. Mun.	Muniments of the Queen's College, Oxford
Red Book Exch.	H. Hall (ed.), *Red Book of the Exchequer* (Rolls Series, 1896)
Regs. Sandale & Asser	F.J. Baigent (ed.), *John de Sandale and Rigaud de Asserio AD 1316-1325. Episcopal Registers: Diocese of Winchester*, (Hampshire Record Society 1897)
Rel. Census 1851	J.A.Vickers, *The Religious Census 1851* (HRS 12, 1993)
Roberts, *Hampshire Houses*	E. Roberts, *Hampshire Houses, 1250–1700: their dating and development*, 2003.
TNA	The National Archives
Valor Eccl.	*Valor Ecclesiasticus*, 6 vols. (Record Commission, 1810–34).
VCH Hants	*The Victoria History of the Counties of England: Hampshire and the Isle of Wight*. Original Editions published 1902–11.
Walker Revised	*Walker Revised*, ed. A.G. Matthews (Oxford, 1948)
WCM	Winchester College Muniments
Reg. Wykeham 1 and 2	T.F. Kirby (ed), *Wykeham's Register, 2 vols.* (HRS, 1896–9)
Youngs, *Admin. Units*, Vol. 1	F.A. Youngs, *Guide to the Local Administrative Units of England, Vol.1, Southern England* (1979)

Page number followed by *n* refers only to the footnotes on that page. Corpus Christi College, Oxford is not given a detailed index; for specific topics relating to the College are referenced individually.

CPSIA information can be obtained
at www.ICGtesting.com
Printed in the USA
FSHW021258310321
79947FS